Crossroads

Guidance for Living

Daily readings based on the sermons of

Dr. Frank N. Kik

Edited by
Doug Pratt and Steven Marsh

Crossroads Guidance for Living
Daily readings based on the sermons of Dr. Frank N. Kik

ISBN 978-1-4507-0317-8

Printed in the United States of America

The Editors wish to express our appreciation to those who have made financial contributions to make possible the printing of this book. All proceeds from its sale will go to mission causes determined by the Sessions of Eastminster Presbyterian Church and First Presbyterian Church of Bonita Springs.

The Publication Team that contributed their expertise to the preparation and printing of this manuscript include: Marilyn Prilliman, Pastor's Executive Assistant at Eastminster Church; Gail Adamo, Publications Director at Eastminster Church; Karis Marsh, Graphic Designer; Donabeth Urick, Pastor's Executive Assistant at First Church; and Gil Urick, gilurickdesign.

Deep gratitude is extended to Dr. Ric Cannada for writing the Foreword, and to the faculty and staff of Reformed Theological Seminary.

And a special word of appreciation is offered to Mrs. Phyllis Kik for her support, advice and counsel on this project – and for trusting the precious legacy of Frank's sermon files and manuscripts to us.

January, 2010

Dr. Douglas Pratt
Senior Pastor
First Presbyterian Church
Bonita Springs, Florida

Dr. Steven Marsh
Senior Pastor
Eastminster Presbyterian Church
Wichita, Kansas

O f all the professors I have been privileged to work with at Reformed Seminary, it is true that I have never received as many letters of appreciation from students as I have concerning Frank Kik. Usually, those letters would come to me long after the students had graduated and would say that they did not appreciate how much Frank had taught them until they were actually seeking to do ministry effectively themselves. Often these graduates would say that they learned more that really helped them in their ministries from Frank Kik than from any other professor.

Frank Kik was a "kick." All who knew him would agree. Although God has created all of us as unique human beings, Frank was seemingly even more so truly one of a kind.

During his more than 10 years as a professor at Reformed Theological Seminary at the campus in Charlotte, NC, Frank made a deep impression on a multitude of preachers and other church leaders who are now serving around the world. He served RTS as a professor of preaching and also as a professor of practical/pastoral theology.

As a professor of preaching, Frank was absolutely committed to the Bible as the Word of God and to the faithful exposition of the Scriptures. He was especially tuned in to the church and the world in our present society and wanted to be sure that our student prospective preachers were being prepared to apply the Scriptures to everyday situations in ways that were clear and effective. He reminded them often that they were preaching to people, not pews.

As a professor of practical/pastoral theology, Frank was as practical as could be possible. He had ministered faithfully and effectively in several churches and had learned well from his successes and from his mistakes. Frank was committed to pass on as much as he could to these student prospective pastors so that they would be effective from the early days of their ministries and would not make the same mistakes that he had made. His workbooks and handbooks on administration and leadership were legendary among the students and covered every conceivable aspect of church leadership, from weddings and funerals and meetings of elders and deacons to how to run a stewardship campaign in the church.

Through it all Frank had a great and unusual sense of humor that showed in everything he taught and did. Although Frank was always fun-loving, he never used his humor at the expense of others. He was thoughtful, sensitive, and kind – a true pastor to his students and in his sermons.

I pray that you will enjoy these messages from Frank and be blessed by them and helped by them in various ways. I hope you also will see and appreciate Frank's personality as you read these messages and get a "kick" out of them for your own spiritual growth and for the good of those around you.

Robert C. Cannada, Jr.
Chancellor and CEO Reformed Theological Seminary

> Here is a trustworthy saying:
> If we died with him,
> we will also live with him;
> if we endure,
> we will also reign with him.
> If we disown him,
> he will also disown us.
>
> 2 Timothy 2:11-12

You have probably heard the story about the man whose death was erroneously reported in the obituary column of the local newspaper. Much enraged he called the editor of the paper and told him, in the words of Mark Twain, that the news of his death had been greatly exaggerated and he insisted that the newspaper print a retraction the very next day. The editor replied, "I'm sorry, but it's been the policy of this newspaper ever since the beginning that once we print something we never retract it. But I'll tell you what I'll do. Tomorrow I'll print your name in the list of *New Births* so you can start all over again."

Inadvertently that story presents for us the central truth of the Christian Gospel – for it's the Gospel of Beginning Again. I'm sure that all of you know that the word "gospel" comes from an old English expression "good spell" which means of course "good news." What is the good news of the Gospel?

I remember that when I was young and jumped rope (you don't see many children jumping rope anymore) we used to have little jingles that we said. Some of you may remember – one, two, three, four, five, six, seven, all good children go to heaven. That was the "Good News." But the industrial revolution, the political revolution, the age of invention, freedom, pleasure, modern comforts and conveniences and recreation began to change all of that. Rightfully, thinking people began to ask: "But isn't there anything good in this life?" Isn't there any "Good News" for today? If life on this earth is totally miserable, corrupted by sin, doomed to disappointment, and the final ignominious defeat is death, then why live it?

But, that wasn't the message of the Master of life. He said, "I have come to give you life and give it to the full." And he wasn't simply talking about "pie in the sky when we die," and we know that. He was talking about life here and now in this world. And we came to the realization through him that we are living eternal life. When? When we get to heaven? Yes, and we are living eternal life now, if we're in Jesus Christ. What, then, is the real message of the Gospel? I like to call it "The Good News of Beginning Again." It's the simple fact that one failure, one tragedy, one loss, one heinous sin, or even a series of such things, doesn't put an end to any hope for life here and now on this earth as well as heaven. Paul, in this second letter to Timothy, reminds us, "Remember Jesus Christ raised from the dead … this is my Gospel. If we died with him, we will also live with him; if we endure, we will also reign with him." Can I start my life over again with a clean slate?

The Bible is full of the Good News of beginning again. Israel – becoming a God-led nation after generations of being just above a mob of motley slaves to the Egyptian empire. Moses – raised up as a spoiled, somewhat aristocratic, hot-headed murderer, a fugitive from justice, begins life again as a great liberator and leader of his people. David – he had real low points, but David rose above his lust, his murder, his adultery and became again the king whom God had appointed. Hosea – betrayed by the woman he'd taken to himself as his wife, goes out and buys her as a prostitute, out of the slave market, takes her home and loves her and they begin again. Certainly in the New Testament we can see the touch of the Master's hand make new people out of many a failure. We've so corrupted the truth of being "born again" that it appears to us now as a lot of theological hodgepodge which nobody understands. But this is what we mean by being born again in Christ: "all things are new" – starting over. Peter – a mouth that always overflowed, a self-styled big shot, a coward, becomes the great hero of the faith as he begins again. James and John – jealous, vindictive, hateful, vengeful, the sons of thunder begin life again as the apostles of love. The adulterous woman – thrown at Jesus' feet with the reminder that the law of the Jews said that she was worthy to be stoned to death hears his gracious words, "Rise and go and sin no more," and begins again. Zacchaeus – a collaborator with Rome, a despised, crooked, vile, tax collector hears the words from the Master, "Today salvation has come to this house," and it had.

> But what about you and your failure? Jesus made one thing clear as the whole Scripture does, "Let the dead past bury its dead." Repent, confess, and go on.

And Zacchaeus and his family began again. Saul – a proud, conceited, arrogant hating Pharisee who had only one answer to anyone who broke the religious law – "Kill him!" – begins again as Paul, the little one, the chief of sinners and becomes the greatest messenger of the Gospel in all of history. No matter how hopeless life may be, no matter what failure, in Christ we have the power to begin again.

I remember Charles Colson telling his story of being counsel to the President of the United States, yet sitting in the driveway of the home of the President of Raytheon, crying his eyes out because he was lost and how he's found and has begun again. And so it is, wherever the gospel touches. The opportunity of beginning again comes with it. This is the gospel of beginning again.

But what about you and your failure? Jesus made one thing clear as the whole Scripture does, "Let the dead past bury its dead." Repent, confess, and go on. No man who puts his hand to the plow and looks back at the mistakes he made is worthy of the Kingdom of God. Paul writes "forgetting those things that are behind I press toward the mark of the high calling in Christ Jesus." In the Lord Jesus Christ we can face tomorrow, because our sins are all gone."

That's the heart of beginning again. Would you want to live constantly with all the mistakes and sins of the past? You couldn't bear it. I couldn't either. That's the heart of the Gospel of beginning again. Hear and believe the Good News. "Be of good cheer. Your sins are forgiven." Begin again. The saying is sure, "If we died with him, we will also live with him."

Father, I am so thankful that I can begin again. That is true by placing one's faith in Jesus Christ as Savior and Lord. I forget what lies behind and press on for the prize. Thank you, Jesus, for forgiving me. In the name of Jesus Christ I pray, Amen.

✳

> When Pharaoh let the people go, God did not lead
> them on the road through the Philistine country,
> though that was shorter ... So God led the people
> around by the desert road toward the Red Sea.

Exodus 13:17-18

In this text of sacred scripture we find a story that lights up an experience common to all of us. It's a familiar life problem with which, sooner or later, we all have to deal: the long way around.

It was only 200 miles from Egypt to Canaan: ten days' journey by camel caravan, and a mere thirty minutes today by airplane. Just 200 miles from the place of slavery to the Land of Promise, yet it took the Israelites forty years to get there. I wonder if this hasn't something very real to say to us in our pilgrimage. "God led them the long way around."

The Bible is called "the book of life" because it speaks honestly to life as it really is. It reminds us of what our experiences confirm. Life is not a smooth path where we can get where we want to go quickly. And it isn't always a straight path. A straight line, our geometry books once told us, is the shortest distance between two points. But that's no longer true even in geometry, since Mr. Einstein challenged Mr. Euclid. It was never true of the progress of the soul. You and I, like those people long ago, are often confronted with the necessity of going the long way around.

Why did it take the people of Israel so long to reach the Promised Land? Because they weren't ready for it. They were slave people with slave minds. And if God had quickly delivered them to the land of their desires without a struggle or scratch, they would be slaves still. Promised lands can't be entered too quickly, before we're ready for them. It's been proven over and over: that which we gain too easily or reach too quickly we esteem too lightly. Promised lands have to be prepared for, worked for, waited for, and deeply wanted. The time in the wilderness was essential time, not wasted time.

I suspect that many of our disappointments in life come from grasping too eagerly for fruit that isn't ripe. We're in a hurry; God isn't. We're petulant; He's patient. We like the shortcut; God takes the long way around. It would help us all to regularly remember that His timetable is not ours. When we sit beside a vast ocean shore, or look up at majestic mountains, we're reminded of how long it took God to fashion our world. He didn't wave a magician's wand. He took the long way around.

> If you find yourself now in some kind of wilderness – whether it's a spell of sickness or a broken plan that makes no sense – maybe you are where God can teach you something.

The world we live in, the world the advertisers are selling, is filled with lies. There certainly are things that we can get immediately today, by pushing the right buttons, by taking the right pills, by putting some money on the counter (or swiping a piece of plastic). But personality can't be purchased. Life skills can't be mastered in one easy lesson. You may acquire a house on easy payments, but it still takes a heap of living in a house to make it a home. No matter what the real estate people say, you can't buy a home. You can only buy a house … and then pitch in and try, with prayer and love and elbow grease, to make it into what you really long for. A true home is not purchased with money, but with tears and sweat and laughter. Cadillacs and Mercedes you can buy with easy down payments, but character and spiritual maturity are things that we earn through our time in the wilderness.

If you find yourself now in some kind of wilderness – whether it's a spell of sickness or a broken plan that makes no sense – maybe you are where God can teach you something. Maybe you are where you can be quiet enough to listen and humble enough to learn.

> *I asked God for strength that I might achieve;*
> *I was made weak that I might learn to obey.*
> *I asked for help that I might do great things;*
> *I was given infirmity that I might do better things.*
> *I asked for riches that I might be happy;*
> *I was given poverty that I might be wise.*
> *I got nothing that I asked for,*
> *but everything I hoped for.*
> *Almost despite myself,*
> *my deepest prayer was answered.*

And so it is: God led the people not by the near way, which they wanted, but by the long way around, which they needed.

> *Lord, I acknowledge my impatience and my selfish lack of trust. I want things the quick and easy way. I realize, though, that Your ways are different from my ways. Help me to trust in You, even when You take me the long way around to get to my destination. Amen.*

❋

Indignant because Jesus
had healed on the Sabbath,
the synagogue ruler said to the people,
"There are six days for work.
So come and be healed on those days,
not on the Sabbath."

Luke 13:14

Isn't it true that whenever you are trying to do something significant, somebody comes around to criticize? Busybodies. Well-known columnist James J. Kilpatrick bought a computer program that not only could scan his copy for errors, but could also tell him about grammar usage, style and punctuation. In short, the computer could tell Kilpatrick the difference between good writing and bad. Just for fun, he fed it some of his own copy and the machine promptly told him he was a lousy writer. Then Kilpatrick tried Lincoln's Gettysburg Address. The computer informed him that Abe's style was very weak because he was wordy and used too much of the passive voice. It also observed that Lincoln used too many adjectives, that most of his sentences contained multiple clauses and that he should try to write more simply.

Even computers are becoming busybodies. Critics are everywhere. Anybody who tries to do anything significant in the world is going to have someone there telling him that he should have done it differently. As American philosopher Yogi Berra once said, "Anyone who is popular is bound to be disliked."

Jesus healed a woman with a bad back. She had been bent over for eighteen years, unable to straighten herself up. Jesus saw her, had compassion on her, and healed her. That's what Jesus does. He heals people. He heals them spiritually, he heals them emotionally and, occasionally, he heals them physically.

There was an article in the newspapers recently about a woman with a chronic bone problem who could not raise her head or drink a cup of tea. She suffered from a rare condition that had caused her head to be stuck pointing down, almost fused to her chest. She was virtually a recluse. Because she couldn't look up, she couldn't safely cross the road. She couldn't eat or drink properly. But she found someone who could help her. You will not believe how. A surgeon used a radical procedure in which he completely detached her head from her spinal column. The story sounds like it was lifted from the *National Enquirer* rather than the Associated Press, but that is the technique he used. At one point, her head was only connected to her shoulders by major arteries and the spinal cord and muscles. After making the necessary adjustments, the surgeon reattached her head to her spine. It was a risky procedure, but it worked. Now she has almost full use of her head and neck. The woman found the right doctor and he healed her.

Two thousand years ago, there were no doctors to perform radical procedures like that. But there was still help. Jesus was there. And Jesus heals people. He healed people then and he heals people now. We are glad that medical science is finally catching on to what you and I have known all our lives. Jesus heals people. He heals them spiritually, he heals them emotionally and, occasionally, he heals them physically. That's what Jesus does.

But still there are critics. Naysayers. Busybodies. There was a critic present when Jesus healed the woman with the bad back. The ruler of the synagogue where Jesus was teaching that day was "moved with indignation" because Jesus healed this woman on the Sabbath. "There are six days in which men ought to work," this ecclesiastical busybody said, "come and be healed on any of those days, but not on the Sabbath." The ruler of the synagogue was upset because Jesus was breaking the rules. "We have a rule," he intoned. "No healing on the Sabbath." Have you ever noticed how many stupid things are done because there are rules?

> That is a lesson that we all need to learn, isn't it? Jesus broke the rules. He healed a woman on the Sabbath. Jesus wanted us to see that God's love for God's children is greater than adherence to rules and laws. We need no longer sit out in the cold, dark night of fear. God's love is greater than all our sin.

Jesus healed a woman with a bad back. Jesus was criticized because this was on the Sabbath. But Jesus answered his critic. He called him a hypocrite. He noted that people will untie their ox or their donkey and lead them to water on the Sabbath. Would they begrudge it that this woman who had been bound for eighteen years should be set free?

In performing this miracle, Jesus established a principle that needs to be engraved on your heart and mind: rules and regulations are important, but the only thing that really matters to God is people. Do you hear what I am saying? It is the message of the gospel. The only thing God really cares about is people.

Not rules. Not laws. People. The reason God gave us laws was for our benefit. This is the way to live life to the fullest, follow these rules. But what if we break one of the rules? It's not the end of the world. There is the healing of forgiveness.

That is a lesson that we all need to learn, isn't it? Jesus broke the rules. He healed a woman on the Sabbath. Jesus wanted us to see that God's love for God's children is greater than adherence to rules and laws. We need no longer sit out in the cold, dark night of fear. God's love is greater than all our sin. All that matters to God is that we come home. And how about you? Are you sitting outside of God's love afraid to come in because you know you've broken the rules and the Lord won't heal you? Come to Jesus. He has paid the penalty for you on the cross and He will heal you. His love and forgiveness is greater than all your broken rules.

Father, thank you for your forgiveness through Jesus Christ. Give me courage to keep believing when the busybodies criticize me for my wrongdoings and tell me that you do not care about me anymore. I love you, Jesus. Heal me this day. In Jesus' name I pray, Amen.

✳

Each heart knows its own bitterness,
and no one else can share its joy.

Proverbs 14:10

A French philosopher said, "The whole world is on a mad quest for happiness." A former president of Harvard said, "The world is searching for a creed to believe and a song to sing." A Texas millionaire confided, "I thought money could buy me happiness, and I have been miserably disillusioned." A famous film star broke down in tears. "I have money, beauty, glamour and popularity. I should be the happiest woman in the world, but I am miserable. Why?" One of the highest people in British social circles lamented, "I have lost all desire to live, yet I have everything to live for. What is the matter with me?"

Our world rushes on in its quest for the fountain of happiness. But the more leisure and pleasure we enjoy, the less satisfied and contented we seem to be. So the search goes on. Inside us a little voice whispers that we were not meant to live this way, that we were meant for greater things. Somewhere, we keep hoping, is the fountain that bubbles up with the happiness that makes life worth living.

The Christian faith is not incompatible with the pursuit of happiness. In fact, its express purpose is to lead us to that true joy that is everlasting. In spite of the false caricatures offered through the years, the truth is that Christianity is a religion of joy. Jesus was so joyful that He called Himself the Bridegroom of the world. He began his teaching in the Sermon on the Mount by pointing the way to true "blessedness," the ultimate condition of lasting joy. And even the night before His crucifixion, He told His disciples, "These things I have said to you that my joy might remain in you, and your joy might be full."

There are far-reaching spiritual laws that govern the human search for happiness – just as every other part of this magnificent universe operates according to the laws laid out by its Creator. True joy is not haphazard or accidental, any more than rain and wind are. It comes to us for a reason. In fact, it is a by-product of other things. When we pursue happiness and try to pounce on it, it eludes us. But when we pursue other things, we find joy as well – a serendipity, a great discovery. Here are three biblical sources of true joy.

1. Happiness comes from inner peace. It is not dependent on our outer circumstances. This is what our Proverb is telling us: both bitterness and joy spring from our inner hearts. And throughout scripture we are pointed to the way to inner peace. It comes from surrendering to the Lord and trusting in Him completely. "My peace I give you," Jesus said. "Not as the world gives give I unto you."

2. Happiness is a by-product of holiness. The word "holy" frightens and intimidates some Christians today, who think it refers to other-worldly saints untouched by normal life. But another way to understand holiness is "wholeness" – being a complete person, with the spiritual dimension to life added to the mental and physical and emotional dimensions. Happiness comes from experiencing fulfillment in our whole, entire selves. This is why those who seek happiness only through sensual pursuits are always disappointed in the end: they have neglected the rest of themselves.

3. Happiness is a consequence of usefulness. This is the small key that unlocks the large door. The Christian faith whispers to us the subtle discovery that the highest human happiness is found in activities which the self-seekers would consider absurd: self-forgetful devotion to something beyond the self. You lose your life to find it. You make yourself useful to God and others and you stop thinking about yourself – and suddenly you discover a joy beyond your expectation. Wilfred Grenfell warned about living life like a barnacle. When they are born in seawater, little barnacles show great promise of being free-swimming animals. But very early they learn to attach themselves to the bottom of boats or to pilings, grow a hard shell on the outside, and spend the rest of their lives hanging on and kicking food into their mouths with their hind legs. A life of freedom becomes enslaved to their attachments. They are useful to no one. Don't be a self-absorbed barnacle, Grenfell pleaded. Give yourself freely to others, and God will cause joy and fulfillment to flow back into your heart.

God, keep reminding me that the way to true and lasting happiness does not lead through selfishness but surrender. I want to give my whole life to Jesus my Lord, that He might give me His joy in return. Amen.

✳

"But even if he does not, we want you to know,
O king, that we will not serve your gods
or worship the image of gold you have set up."

Daniel 3:18

It's refreshing to meet men and women who have souls. In our
Scripture lesson Nebuchadnezzar, King of Babylon, has set up
in the plain of Dura a great image 90 feet high. It's an image
adorned with gold which represents the god of his empire's proud
success. He commands that all people shall come and bow down
before the image. But three young Jews, captives in Babylon,
refuse to worship this pagan god of the King. Nebuchadnezzar's
furious. He threatens that they shall be thrown alive into the
furnace which was kept for cremating dead bodies. However,
Shadrach, Meshach and Abednego won't flinch from their refusal
to bow down to his image.

It is difficult to count the people today who regulate their
principles by the going price who can't decide a question of
right or wrong without consulting the political polls nor conclude
what they ought to do until they've ascertained what it is for their
interest to do. In the great world war between sin and holiness
many are attempting to see which side is going to win and they
help the successful side and plunder whichever is defeated.
Shadrach, Meshach and Abednego were not shells of men, but
real men who had souls. They really believed that there is a right
and wrong; that the right was to be done even if it would cost
one's life.

The world resounds with whining over difficulties. The high school student crying about his French. The girl complaining about her boyfriend. Teenagers bellyaching that their parents don't want them to have any friends to adults crying about their jobs and how hard they have to work. And it's sad that men and women complain more childishly of their difficulties in their religious commitment. Those who wouldn't even be suspected of fearing obstacles in their business, who love even to meet and overcome them will shrink away from encountering difficulties in the way of serving the Lord and even deem them an ample apology for not serving God.

They seem even to think that these dreams of what they would do if it could work out constitute a sort of virtue and their dreams become their faith before God. Difficulties? It's impossible to be real men and women without them. What would a young man of 21 who'd never encountered any difficulties be worth, who had almost everything handed over to him on a silver platter? He would simply be an overgrown baby. His passions, his emotions might be gigantic while his personality would be puny and undeveloped. Why are so many of you real women and real men? You met many difficulties while young.

God educates us by difficulties. Shadrach, Meshach and Abednego's problems weren't composed of afflictions, pain, hatred, war. They resided in an affluent and idolatrous community and in many ways they had it made. Life could be easy … they were surrounded by all the luxuries, gaieties and allurements of a king's palace. Yet they chose to serve the Lord. They didn't waste time crying over their difficulties. Difficulties constitute the school by which we're educated.

God will rescue us from the furnace. It's a natural thing for men and women, if we want a faith at all, to want a faith which seems to work. Our philosophy is something like this: If we worship God, then God will take care of his worshipers. Our human nature demands that religion ought to bring obvious benefits. If a woman follows after goodness, then the result ought to be good. If she's righteous, then the plain issues of her life ought to turn out right. If we trust God, then he'd better show up when we need him. We want to be sure that his help is real when things get difficult.

Take the ordinary things of life. Watch men and women in the business world. It may be they've started with high Christian ideals. Men and women who've grown up in Christian homes, taught in Christian Sunday schools, worshiped faithfully in God's house and then they go out into the competitive struggle of the commercial life. They soon realize that in this new world of theirs there is another god besides the God they were earlier taught to worship. It's the gilded god which the Nebuchadnezzars of our modern Babylons have set up, the god of ambition, riches and success.

Let's imagine a modern person in the midst of a modern Babylon, facing the same dilemma the three men in the Book of Daniel faced. This man wants to have faith on Sundays, but things are different on Mondays. He wishes that God would spare him from the pressure to worship a golden idol. He wishes that God would allow him to make money and get ahead rapidly while still keeping his faith. But when he finds himself facing a conflict between his spiritual values on one side and his material fortune on the other, what shall he do?

Does real faith hold out in times of crisis? I can't promise you a painless life. There are times, more often than we like, when we must sacrifice and lose money, possessions, jobs, friendships, the joy of powerful and successful interests, rather than sell our souls. We must be willing, as these men in Babylon were, to go straight into the furnace of affliction, rather than submit to the idol which will crush out the dignity of our life.

In the loneliness of his own conviction Martin Luther faced the Holy Roman Emperor Charles IV and said, "My cause shall be commended to the Lord for he lives and reigns who preserved the three young men in the furnace of the Babylonian King. If he is willing to preserve me, my life is a small thing compared with Christ's who was wickedly slain to the disgrace of all and the harm of many. Expect anything of me except flight or recantation. I will not run, much less recant. So may the Lord Jesus strengthen me."

Will someone be here 100 years from now because of what you did in your sphere of influence? It's great to meet men and women who have souls.

Almighty God, you are with me in the furnaces of life. Thank you that you promise to sustain us even in suffering. Thank you that you promise that all things will work for the good of those who love you. May I find strength in you, Jesus, this day in whatever I face, may I be a witness of loving you in the pain. In the name of Jesus Christ I pray, Amen.

✳

Jesus made His disciples get into the boat
and go on ahead of Him. After leaving them,
He went up on a mountainside to pray …
When evening came,
the boat was in the middle of the lake,
and the wind was against them.
He went out to them, walking on the lake.
Immediately he spoke to them and said,
"Take courage! It is I. Don't be afraid."
Then He climbed into the boat with them,
and the wind died down.

Mark 6:45-50

The story of Jesus walking on the water to come to the aid of His disciples has always stirred human souls. The episode took place immediately after the feeding of the five thousand. Jesus then sent the crowds away, and commanded His disciples to get into their boat and go off without Him. The Lord needed some solitude and some time to pray.

What a perfect example He provides to us. William Penn once wrote: "Till we are persuaded to stop and step aside out of the prospect of things, it will be impossible to make a right adjustment of ourselves. The wise man is he who from time to time withdraws from the crowd and looks at it from the standpoint of the eternal." The Lord did this continually throughout His ministry. Even before the crucible of the cross He spent moments of solitude in Gethsemane.

Meanwhile, the disciples start out on what they expect will be a smooth trip across a glassy lake. But suddenly a storm swept down on them. Their boat was tossed about in a turbulent and angry sea. They began to panic. Why did this storm come upon them? They had not embarked on some foolish or hasty enterprise. They were doing what their Lord had told them to do – and this was their reward for obedience?

We could conclude that the storm came randomly. Certainly we observe that both the righteous and the wicked experience storms; as Jesus said elsewhere, God "makes rain fall on the just and the unjust." We know that faith is not a blanket protection policy, guaranteeing we will never face storms in life. It's true that some storms come from our own willful actions and mistakes. And some are caused by the fault of others. And still others are sent to us providentially by God to shake us out of our complacency. But in all cases, storms can be turned into strengthening agents for those who believe.

> Though He was in deep and sweet communion with His Heavenly Father, Jesus was not so absorbed that He failed to see the distress of His friends. He came to them in their crisis. God is not so busy today driving the car of the universe that He fails to notice the pedestrians walking the face of the earth.

Many times it is through difficulties and obstacles that we really grow. As it was said, "the north wind made the Vikings." The most important truth for us to grasp is that the presence and power of God are available to us in the midst of the storm.

Though He was in deep and sweet communion with His Heavenly Father, Jesus was not so absorbed that He failed to see the distress of His friends. He came to them in their crisis. God is not so busy today driving the car of the universe that He fails to notice the pedestrians walking the face of the earth. Scripture assures me and you that He still walks to us over the waters of our troubles to guide us through the storms that blow on us.

Why did this storm come upon me? We may not know for a long time, or even in our earthly lifetimes. But it's not important to know why. The most important question is: Where is God in the storm? The answer scripture gives to us: He is coming to us, if we have eyes to see Him, and He wants to step into our little boats and bring His calm and peace.

Lord, at times I feel tossed about by life's events. I feel so helpless, and I am reminded of my need for you. Please come to me in my storm, and bring to me your peace. Amen.

✳

But grow in the grace and knowledge
of our Lord and Savior Jesus Christ.
To him be glory both now and forever!
Amen.

2 Peter 3:18

Growth is a transformation of one form of energy and matter into another. Living things are by definition transformers of energy and matter. Certain anatomical structures are found at all or most stages of development.

In its earliest developmental state the human being is a one-celled organism; by early adulthood it has become an organism of more than 20 trillion cells. At birth a man's body length is about 4 times the length of his face so that his head is relatively large. In the course of development his head grows relatively slower than his trunk and limbs. At about 25, man's body length is approximately 8 times the length of his face. Growth may continue from birth to death as in most plants and in some animals such as crocodiles and turtles; or it may be confined to certain growth periods in the development of the individual, as in most animals and in man. While many mammals get their growth in 1 or 2 years, man goes on growing until he is about 30.

Moral and religious growth begins at the age of 1 or 2. Man's ability to walk and talk and his increasing control of hands and arms, make possible greatly increased interaction with other persons and increased participation in the common consciousness of the family. At this time he acquires many likings that he feels, but cannot explain in later life. If the persons around him show fear of worms, insects, snakes, darkness, lightning, he shows their feelings and may in later life be unable to overcome his timidity, although he knows that there is absolutely no basis in reason or fact for such feelings.

Throughout the New Testament, Christian character is regarded as growth. Sometimes the growth is architectural such as the growth of a building (chief cornerstone); sometimes it is physiological, Christ being the head, and we growing up into Him in all things; sometimes it is generic growth, as in the case of the vine which brings forth more and more fruit under pruning and culture.

My father once said to me, after many years of experience, "I am never too old to learn and grow. I learn something almost every day." He was a man of vast knowledge. After his death a friend told me that he had said that if he were to write down on paper all that he knew, it would take him 10 years. But he learned something new every day.

At times we who are younger feel that it is no longer necessary to grow. Sometimes when we find ourselves in difficulty of sickness and trial we feel that we are nearing the end of life and there is no need of seeking to grow.

Simon Peter had a battle with this question in life. When he was younger he felt that he knew it all and could always be the spokesman of the group. Now that he had become older and had wisdom in Christian experience he wrote to the strangers of the dispersed (Gentiles) that the purpose of his very existence was to grow in the grace of Christ. "But grow in grace, and in the knowledge of our Lord and Savior Jesus Christ."

Now, the text does not mean grow into the grace or into the knowledge. It means, being in grace – grow; being in the knowledge of our Lord Jesus Christ – grow. We are to grow in both grace and knowledge. This is clear when we read verse 17 as well as 18. "Ye therefore, beloved, knowing these things beforehand, beware lest, being carried away with the error of the wicked, ye fall from your own steadfastness. But grow in the grace and knowledge of our Lord and Savior Jesus Christ." The negative command: "Beware lest ye fall." The positive command: "Knowing these things, grow in the grace and knowledge." You are in the grace now – grow; knowledge now – grow.

The figure is that of infancy advancing to the full stature of manhood. The gods of the ancients were born full-grown. Minerva is said to have sprung all armed and panoplied from the forehead of Jove. But Christians begin as babes in Christ and advance through certain conditions of normal growth to the "measure of the stature of the fullness of Christ."

The grace of God. The grace of Jesus is the graciousness, the gentleness, the harmony of life in God and in his Son. We have the grace of our Lord, the undeserved love and favor which God in Christ gives to us sinful and inferior creatures and next, we have the consequences of that love and favor in the spiritual gifts which become a part of our personality.

> The knowledge of God. To know more of Jesus is to know more of God. The life of Christ is a reflection of God.

The knowledge of God. To know more of Jesus is to know more of God. The life of Christ is a reflection of God. And the more we know of him we then learn what things God approves. And we cannot grow in our spiritual lives unless we gain more knowledge of him.

Growth is dependent upon life and health. Grant these conditions and growth follows naturally and without effort. If these be absent, there can be no growth. It is dependent upon life. You might take a snowball and roll it in the snow and watch it become larger and larger and one might say, "See how it grows," but it is not growing – that is not growth; that is enlargement by accretion from without. Growth is enlargement by development from within.

Wherever there is the stunting of growth in the Christian life, it is because some part of the intellect, emotion, will, imagination or affection is not wholly surrendered to the indwelling Christ. The tides of that life that are excluded from some part of Jesus' claims will result in spiritual disease. The spiritual faculties become wasted – they cannot work. And then spiritual growth is stunted. In a word, we live in him and the measure in which he nourishes us is at once the measure of our health, strength and our life. Let us confess the aspects of our spiritual growth which are functioning as dwarfs; and for those parts which are functioning as giants, let us praise God. Let us trust God for the growth as we continue to move from dwarfs to giants in the faith.

Father, help me to admit those aspects of my life that I have become content in their dwarf development. Give me the courage to grow into a giant of faith. May God's grace and knowledge be sufficient for that growth. In the name of Jesus I pray, Amen.

✻

Listen! A farmer went out to sow his seeds …
Still other seed fell on good soil.
It came up, grew and produced a crop,
multiplying thirty, sixty, or even a hundred times.

Mark 4:3, 8

Jesus told a parable about a sower who went forth to sow seed. Not all the seed germinated. Some of it was soon eaten by birds. Other seed had a short life, and then quickly died before fruit was produced. But some seed, falling on receptive soil, produced an abundant harvest. I can imagine people listening to Jesus' words and then muttering, "What in the world is He talking about?" They had come to Him to hear profound theological preaching, and all they got were simple homespun stories. Jesus knew His listeners' hearts, and He was not concerned. Because He knew that a few of them would respond in ways that would change them forever.

The parable of the sower calls us to make a choice. What kind of life shall we live? Shall we live only for ourselves? Or shall we devote ourselves to the pursuit of living fruitful lives?

Mother Teresa once made a choice. She didn't set out to help the poor. For over twenty years she taught the wealthiest children in the finest parochial school in Calcutta. Every day she overlooked the impoverished slums and the people living in the streets that surrounded the well-to-do neighborhood in which she worked. She was perfectly content with her life, until one night. While walking home, she heard a woman crying out for help. Realizing the seriousness of the woman's condition, Mother Teresa rushed her to the nearest hospital. At the hospital she was told to sit and wait. Nothing happened … urgently needed medical care was denied, all because the sick woman belonged to the wrong social caste. In desperation, Mother Teresa took the woman to her home. Later that night the woman died in the comfort of Mother Teresa's loving arms. That night the nun resolved that this would never happen again to anyone within her reach. She decided she would devote her life to easing the pain of those who suffered around her. Whether they lived or died, they would do so with dignity. Mother Teresa made a choice that night. She never dreamed that because of it, her name would become a household word. We never know, when we're sowing seed, what the result might be.

> The seed of God's Word has that kind of effect in hearts made fertile and ready for it. That is why those who work in service to the Lord never lose heart. The seeds we sow may seem tiny and insignificant. But at harvest time the yield is amazing.

All it takes is fertile and receptive ground. A farmer using the methods Jesus described in His parable might normally expect a yield of anywhere between seven and ten times. There would be some loss along the way, but such a yield could sustain the farmer and provide the seed for the next year's planting. But something about the seed in this story has a supernatural power within it, the power to produce a stunning and tremendous harvest. The seed of God's Word has that kind of effect in hearts made fertile and ready for it. That is why those who work in service to the Lord never lose heart. The seeds we sow may seem tiny and insignificant. But at harvest time the yield is amazing.

Years ago, soon after the peaceful end of Communism in Russia, Boris Yeltsin was interviewed by a western reporter. When asked what gave him the courage to stand firm, he credited the story he'd read of Lech Walesa, the electrician who helped bring democracy to Poland. Similarly, Walesa has stated that he was inspired by reading accounts of the civil rights movement in this country led by Martin Luther King. And Dr. King testified that he was stirred to action when he learned of the courage of a little woman named Rosa Parks, who refused to sit in the back of the bus. We seldom know the potential of the seed we sow. But it's possible that the fall of Communism was brought about by one black woman who had enough self-respect to say no to prejudice. You and I never know, when we say or do something inspired by our Lord, what the effects will be. Perhaps today you can plant a seed in someone's heart that will bring forth an abundant harvest.

Lord, only You can prepare another's heart to receive the truth. And only You know what the results of my life will be. Help me to take up the sacred calling this day to plant seeds, and to trust You for the harvest. Amen.

✳

"… in quietness and trust is your strength,
but you would have none of it."

Isaiah 30:15b

You need no word from me to emphasize why in the tenseness of our times people everywhere are seeking some measure of inner stability. We're living in a decade in which we've seen a deepening of almost every major problem. While the crime rate is decreasing, brutality is increasing. Dragging a man behind a truck until he's dead, the stoning of a man because he is a homosexual, the dismembering of a woman's body while she is still alive. The dehumanizing of life is at an extreme point. Most of us have come to terms with the probability that we shall have to live for the rest of our days in a time of trouble and anxiety. That great Christian statesman, Dr. Elton Trueblood, stated, "Whatever the course of history may be in the next years, it will not be a course of tranquility." Our modern world has developed so much animosity, so much justifiable fear, so much open conflict, that there is no peace. Peace in our time is as unlikely as was prosperity in the South immediately after the American Civil War. Instead of pining for calmer days, the way of wisdom is to learn to live wisely and well in the midst of continuous strain.

In our Scripture, Israel always felt the difficulty of sustaining itself on the height of dependence on the unseen spiritual power of God and was ever oscillating between alliances with the northern and southern powers, linking itself with Assyria against

Egypt or with Egypt against Assyria. The Prophet's warning was political wisdom as truly as spiritual. Here Judah is exhorted to forsake the entangling dependence on Egypt and to trust wholly on God. They'd departed from him in their fears, they must come back by their faith. To them the great lesson was trust in God. Through them, to us, the same lesson is read. The principle is far wider than this one case. It's the rule of life for us all. When the Bible talks about inner stability (and it talks a good deal about it, though I doubt if the word itself ever appears) it presents it as an intensely spiritual achievement. How do we achieve the dignity of inner stability in the midst of continuing strain?

First of all we must have a right perspective. That is, we must have the ability to see the present moment, which is an immediate event, against the background of a larger reference. One reason we get fidgety about our time is that we stand too close to it and we're too much of a part of it to see it in its proper perspective. I can't understand this time, except in relation to the total purposes of God as revealed in his cross. An occasional brush with failure, or sorrow, or bereavement is sure to come. When we stand too close to it, a six-foot grave can fill the whole earth. We need perspective, even in the small annoyances of everyday relationships. How a trivial disagreement can take the foreground as though it were a world-shaking calamity.

The second ingredient of inner poise is balance – emotional balance. That isn't quite the same thing as perspective. It's the restraint and control of runaway emotion. While our emotions are the driving force of life, when they get out of hand they can destroy us. One of the sinister marks of our time is extremism. Emotional forces out of balance. Loud angry voices shouting at each other across fences. Some real and some imaginary without regard to accuracy, without the restraint of reason. The whole country today seems in an ugly mood as if we'd all been suddenly bitten by the same venomous bug. Black against white, white against black, husband against wife, wife against husband, Democrats against Republicans. Union against management, management against Union. Pro-life against pro-choice, pro-gambling against no gambling. Sexual preference and no preference. Everybody rallies around his hates. Christians should be a healing influence in society. The great destroyer of inner stability is inner conflict and runaway emotion.

> When you have a thought-out faith like that, you're not likely to be upset by doubts, confusions, controversies, contradictions, or even by opposition. Don't pray for easy lives, pray to be stronger women and men. Don't pray for tasks equal to your powers. Pray for powers equal to your tasks.

Kipling has said it well: "If you can keep your head when all about you are losing theirs and blaming it on you; if you can trust yourself when all men doubt you, but make allowances for their doubting too; if you can wait and not be tired by waiting or being lied about, don't deal in lies, or being hated, don't give way to hating, and yet don't look too good nor talk too wise; if you can dream and not make your dreams your master; if you can think and not make thoughts your aim; if you can meet with triumph and disaster and treat those two impostors just the same; if you can bear to hear the truth you've spoken twisted by knaves to make a trap for fools; or watch the things you gave your life to

broken, and stoop and build 'em up with worn-out tools …"
That's it, the balance of emotion.

I'm convinced that there is nothing that can give confidence
or perspective and balanced emotion than the assurance that
you're standing on solid ground. In the words of the hymn
writer: "My hope is built on nothing less than Jesus' blood and
righteousness. I dare not trust the sweetest frame, but wholly
lean on Jesus' name. On Christ the solid rock I stand, all other
ground is sinking sand, all other ground is sinking sand." When
you have a thought-out faith like that, you're not likely to be upset
by doubts, confusions, controversies, contradictions, or even by
opposition. Don't pray for easy lives, pray to be stronger women
and men. Don't pray for tasks equal to your powers. Pray for
powers equal to your tasks.

"In quietness and trust is your strength." That's in the 30th
chapter of Isaiah. If it's to be in the chapter ahead of us we
will have to work it out: by perspective, setting this moment in
its larger reference and by balance, the restraint and control
of runaway emotions. You can live wisely and well in a time of
continuing strain.

For perspective and balance of emotion I pray, oh God.
May your promises sustain me. May I find my strength in you.
It is in the name of Jesus Christ I pray, my strength,
Rock and Redeemer. Amen.

✳

I urge you, brothers, in view of God's mercy,
to present your bodies as living sacrifices,
holy and pleasing to God – this is your
spiritual act of worship.

Romans 12:1

I remember the old *Saturday Evening Post* magazine, with its memorable covers illustrated by Norman Rockwell. The scenes were so familiar and homey, the stuff that most of our lives are made of. Nothing much important happened in those pictures – just ordinary people going through the ordinary motions of living. One cynic labeled the subjects of Rockwell's work "Insignificance U.S.A."

Ouch! It's painful to think that our lives might fit that description. And yet, it feels that way at times: we become slaves to endless routines; the weeks and months and years race by, and we wonder if we have anything significant to show for them. We immerse ourselves in the tasks of life. We run and run, busier and busier. The rabbit said to Alice in Wonderland, "You always have to run faster when you don't know where you're going." That's what a life of insignificance feels like.

But our text for today speaks to our deep longing for lives of significance – and it points the way to finding it. "Present your bodies as living sacrifices … this is your spiritual act of worship." This is God's call to step out of the endless race, the cycle of insignificance, and find a lasting meaning and purpose. "Called out" from the crowd is our identity. The original word for "church" literally means "those who are called out." He has called us out for a purpose.

The story of God's Word is the story of common, ordinary, seemingly-insignificant people who had never done anything out of the ordinary in their lives. Many of them were middle-aged or old, many of them were just from the poor or middle class, and they all had their excuses. Some couldn't speak well, weren't very gifted, or didn't come from royal blood. And, almost without exception, when God called them their response was disbelief. Who, me? They were completely astounded at what the Lord was able to make out of their lives. The key was not their ability but their availability: they "presented their bodies as living sacrifices," and God used them.

At times, when confronted by the great problems and tragedies of the world, we are tempted to feel overwhelmed. We can't do it all … but God's Spirit whispers to us that we can at least do something. And when we do, as an act of love, obedience and response to God's grace, that task of service has eternal significance.

When we see our lives as being instruments to bring glory to God, we have direction and meaning and purpose. When we don't believe that God wants to use us, then life looks meaningless. The one hope that can save us from a life in residence in "Insignificance U.S.A." is through giving ourselves to a cause that is greater than ourselves. May God help us each to find His purpose for us today, and then to help us place our will on the altar as a living sacrifice!

Deliver me, Lord, from my petty preoccupations and worries. Help me to see the great purpose in all of life: to worship and serve You. I now freely offer myself as a living sacrifice to be used as You wish. Amen.

※

"This, then, is how you should pray:
'Our Father in heaven'"

Matthew 6:9

T hroughout the Christian centuries men have poured forth their hearts to God in these few words that have come to be known as the Lord's Prayer. They have probably had a greater influence on the world than all the writings of theologians put together. They are the simplest form of communion with Christ. When we utter them we are one with him. His thoughts become our thoughts, and we draw near to God through him. They also bind us with our fellow men in which we acknowledge him as our Father and that we are his children. And even the smallest particular of our lives admit of being ranged under one or another of the petitions contained in this prayer and offered up to God.

Contrary to popular feeling, no single petition of this prayer was in the strict sense "original." Almost all these phrases can be found in the prayers of the children of Israel. It would be possible to rewrite the whole of the Lord's Prayer in words taken from the Old Testament. In fact, we could narrow this down just to the Book of Psalms, which is the prayer book of the Bible and echoes not only the words of the Psalms but the music to which they are set.

The startling originality of this prayer is its structure. Within the narrow framework of an utterance containing only petitions, Jesus has gathered all the deepest necessities of man as a whole and as an individual and he has so knit together and built up these petitions in orderly sequence that the prayer as a whole appeals to men everywhere.

Jesus is giving his followers instructions concerning giving to the poor, praying and fasting. And with regard to prayer he says, "When thou prayest, thou shalt not be as the actors, for they love to pray standing in the synagogues and in the corners of the streets, that they may be seen of men." Right things may be done in a wrong way and so may lose their value. It is right to give, right to pray, right to fast, but they may all be done in a wrong way.

Now we cannot really measure our prayers by minutes. No prayer is long that is prayed with the heart; as long as the heart can talk, the prayer is very brief. If you are praying publicly – remember that someone else's heart might not be in tune with yours. Beware of a mechanical piety. To avoid a mechanistic prayer and to be personal, Jesus gives us a short, dramatic, terse and cogent prayer which brings before him all the needs of a man's heart.

"Our Father." The word Father implies personality. He is, therefore, a personal God whom man is to worship. It is not a principle but a person we are to invoke; not nature, but God, "our Father." All worship which loses itself in vague generalities addressed to some great abstraction, or trust in such a thing as men call nature, is at once condemned by the opening words of this prayer. "After this manner, therefore, pray ye," to a living ever-present person; himself moving amid and regulating all his works, not estranging himself from his creation – but a Father ever working through all. You never say Father to a force; Father, to a law; Father, to a mist. The word Father means we are praying to a living person.

In what sense are we the sons and daughters of God? Some say that the fatherhood of God is universal and that every man, from the fact of his being created by God, is necessarily God's son, and that therefore every man has a right to approach the throne of God and say, "Our Father which art in heaven." I must disagree with that statement. I believe that in this prayer we are to come before God, looking upon him not as our Father through creation, but as our Father through adoption and the new birth. Those who can say, "Our Father," are something more than God's creatures: they have been adopted into his family. He has taken sinful men and said, "I will make them my sons." He has washed them and cleansed them. He gives them a new name. No man has the right to claim God as his father unless he feels in his soul and believes, solemnly, through the faith of God's election that he has been adopted into the one family of God which is in heaven and earth.

> Let us who claim the name of Christ, remember to pray to our Father. We are adopted into God's family through Jesus Christ. We have a Father who loves us and whose discipline is for our betterment.

When you think of God the Father, you think of him with fear and trembling. He is such a holy God. He hates sin. You think of him as an angry God and stand in dread of him. You picture him as the great Judge sitting on a throne of judgment welcoming the holy to heaven and sending the wicked to hell. But the thought I wish to impress on your mind is that God is also a father. And if God be Father, he loves me. When God is a friend he is the best of friends and sticks closer than a brother; and when he is a father he is the best of fathers. Fathers, perhaps you do not know how much you love your children. But when they are sick you find that out, for you stand by their beds and you pity them, as their little frames are writhing in pain. Well, "like as a father pitieth his children, so the Lord pitieth them that trust Him." And you know how you love your children, when they grieve you by their sin; anger arises and you are ready to chasten them; but no sooner is the tear in their eye, than your hand is heavy and you feel that you would rather punish yourself than punish them. And such is the case with God, our God even our Father.

Let us who claim the name of Christ, remember to pray to our Father. We are adopted into God's family through Jesus Christ. We have a Father who loves us and whose discipline is for our betterment.

Almighty God, our Father, may your name be praised. I pray now to my Father, the one who knows me, loves me and calls me to a life of faithfulness in his world. May I never take for granted the fatherhood of God. In Jesus' name I pray, Amen.

✳

I sought the LORD, and He answered me;
He delivered me from all my fears.

Psalm 34:4

Hamlet spoke eloquently for the human race when he
declared, "Conscience doth make cowards of us all."
Though Shakespeare wrote long ago in a different age,
even in our modern day of so many creature comforts and blessings
we find that fear can control us and make "cowards of us all."

In my experience as a pastoral counselor I have learned
that fear is prevalent in many hearts. Often people look to a
minister to provide all the answers to the anxieties of life. But I
must confess that this minister doesn't have all the neat and tidy
answers. He, too, struggles with anxieties and fears as a man, a
husband, a father and a provider. He, too, is concerned with bills
and insurance and taxes and retirement savings and health.

Fear is everywhere around us – even all-pervasive. It can seep
into our physical, emotional and spiritual fibers. To paraphrase
Emerson, fear is a circle whose circumference is everywhere
and whose center is nowhere. Fear does not "stand up to be
counted" but operates in disguise. Its greatest potency lies in
being hidden. Often it is completely covered by an outward
stoicism and bravado. But it is there.

The powerful force of fear can be a friend or an enemy
to a Christian, depending on how we deal with it. Indeed,
fear can be the starting point of wisdom. How can fear be a
friend? By warning us of danger and steering us towards right

choices. It can thus be helpful and constructive. Were it not for normal healthy fears, thousands of lives would be lost through carelessness. I do not wish to trust myself to an airline pilot who knows no fear or respect of the power of gravity. I am not willing to take medication prepared by a pharmacist who has no fear of making a mistake and thus is reckless in mixing chemicals. The fear of making an error thankfully keeps many people alert and scrupulous in their work. In hundreds of ways, fear is thus a safeguard to human society.

> In my life I have found it to be absolutely true that when I sincerely put my life in God's hands and trust Him to take care of me, He does so with amazing kindness. This is one of the greatest secrets in the world. It gives peace and strength beyond calculation. Let all your fears go, by giving them to God. He will not let you down.

But when constructive fear becomes exaggerated out of proportion it becomes our destructive enemy. It can control us, intimidate us, dominate us and limit us. In Psalm 34 the poet David is speaking about this kind of fear. And he points the way to the antidote for this poison.

It's not possible to expel from our minds negative and unwholesome fears simply by an act of the will. It is useless to say, "I will not let my mind dwell on these things." They will only return in unguarded moments. But there is another way to deal with fears than by our unaided willpower. A Chicago psychiatrist named Dr. William Sandler put it plainly: "The only known cure for fear is faith."

Christian faith teaches us to say, "No matter what misfortunes come my way, I will look them in the face. I will meet them one-by-one and demonstrate that they are not to be feared, but yielded to the Master."

In my life I have found it to be absolutely true that when I sincerely put my life in God's hands and trust Him to take care of me, He does so with amazing kindness. This is one of the greatest secrets in the world. It gives peace and strength beyond calculation. Let all your fears go, by giving them to God. He will not let you down.

Have you ever carried a tired child in your arms? You remember the complete relaxation of that little body. The child rests in your embrace, entirely free from tension. He does not fear that he will be dropped, for he trusts you. Feeling that trust, you hold the little form all the closer and with greater care, for you do not want to fail such complete confidence. If this kind of love and faith passes between parents and their tired children, how much more profoundly does God take to His heart His human children of all ages who are tired and worn in the dark nights of this life?

Lord, help me to recognize those fears that arise in me that are your word of conscience and warning. And help me also to recognize those fears that are irrational or destructive, and turn them over to you whenever they surface in my mind. I trust that, as I seek you, you will answer me by "delivering me from all my fears." Amen.

✳

Therefore, since we are surrounded
by such a great cloud of witnesses,
let us throw off everything that hinders
and the sin that so easily entangles,
and let us run with perseverance the
race marked out for us. Let us fix our
eyes on Jesus, the author and perfecter
of our faith, who for the joy set before
him endured the cross, scorning its
shame, and sat down at the right hand
of the throne of God.

Hebrews 12:1-2

At the time of the full moon of the month of April in the
year that we now reckon as 776 B.C., a crowd of some
45,000 Greeks seated on the grassy slopes of the
stadium at Olympia rose up and cheered as a naked runner burst
ahead of his rivals on the track and led them across the finish line.
The winner was Coroebus, a cook from the nearby city of Elis.
It was a dash to glory for Coroebus for by winning that race he
became the first victor of record of the Olympic Games. From that
year on the Olympic Games were held every four years for nearly
1,200 years without a single interruption.

The figure that Paul employs in our text is a reference to the
famous Olympic Games which were familiar to all Greek speaking
people. This is the idea that Paul grabs hold of to illustrate our

spiritual experience. Earth, he says, is the arena wherein great things are being accomplished from age to age by the sons and daughters of God.

Life is a race – an individual effort. Every man or woman is what his/her life is and his life is just how he has run his race. The road is hers, the opportunity is hers, the means and instruments are his and if he fails the fault is his. To all alike God gives the race and gives to each the skills for success.

The figure of an Olympian athlete means a life in earnest or it means nothing. Useful service in life or duty well done, that's our goal. Temptation met and resisted and conquered, that's our goal. Temptation met – resisted – conquered, that's our goal. Power to love, to be just, to be pure, to be true, to control external and internal life, that's our goal. The success of the Christian lawyer, teacher, business man and woman, physician, laborer, scholar is just so much power added to the personality which he consecrates to the cause of the Lord and to the uplifting of humanity in the world. We should look upon success in our daily vocation as a duty which we owe to our God. We should work our business, or our study, our practice, our manual labor, until it has become a success. To win the gold in every case will take hard work, but to do hard and healthful work within the will of God is one of the purposes of God in bringing us into the world.

This race is appointed for the follower of Jesus. He also finds that he can't choose his own way to the goal. The race is set before her, marked out for her, measured and staked by a power not her own. His birth, his natural condition, temperament, talents, opportunities are all arranged for him, that's the course set before him or her and you must win the gold by running in that course. He may not leave the lanes and try a shortcut, she may not demand a softer course, he may not ask that the sand be removed and a blacktop surface prepared for him. She may not require that the hills be leveled and rough places be made smooth. She must take the course as she finds it. In other words, we mustn't wait until things are made easier for us. We mustn't refuse to run because the course isn't all we could wish for.

In the race, we are to lay aside every weight. This means that which is superfluous in the case of a runner – unnecessary clothing, or excess body fat, these impede the runner. And as the athlete in the race wears the minimum clothing and keeps her body in shape and submits cheerfully to the trainer's rules, denying herself even the little indulgences which other folk allow themselves, so we mustn't carry an ounce of unnecessary weight. Pleasures, friendships, occupations, habits may in themselves be innocent, but if they hinder our running they must be given up.

There is also the weight of unforgiven sin. You have offended a mother, a father, teacher, friend, you have been guilty of disobedience or untruthfulness or dishonesty … how heavy is it? It lies like lead on your heart. It hinders you in everything you put your hands to do. Or the fault has been discovered and you're in disgrace. Your dearest friends are displeased. You feel as if there's a great gulf between you and them. You're unhappy. What of your temper that bursts into passion on the slightest provocation? What of our pride and vanity? What of our selfishness that disregards others and is always seeking our own gratification and pleasure? What of secret sins which you try to conceal, but which are always growing stronger and if unsubdued will go on as they're doing, burning like a fire within and eating out your very heart and soul? What's to be done with the weight of these sins? "Throw them off." Everything that hinders us in the race must go.

We can't turn to God unless we turn away from evil that hinders us in our race. Coming to the Lord always means leaving something behind that causes us to stumble and fall. Discover what's the weak point in your life and begin to exercise self-control.

We're tempted to look at the thing behind, to consider the difficulties, trials, sorrows, the sins of the past. Remorse bids us catalogue our crimes. Discouragement bids us remember the past obstacles. Unbelief constrains us to believe every tale of all the embarrassment of the past. Look away from the things that are past.

The joy of victory lies before us, not the agony of defeat. Go for it my friends. Go for the gold in your spiritual life. God hasn't called you to lose the race. God hasn't called you to failure. He wants on that final great day to give you the gold. Might we be able to say at the closing ceremony: I have fought the good fight; I have finished the race; I have kept the faith; now there is in store for me the crown of righteousness.

Father, thank you for showing us the way to run the race.
We see that design most fully as we look at the life of Jesus.
May we run with perseverance and joy; confidence and trust.
Thank you for loving me as your child. I will run the race
with boldness. And I pray these things in the strong name
of Jesus Christ my Savior. Amen.

*

I pray that you, being rooted and established in love,
may have power, together with all the saints,
to grasp how wide and long and high and deep is
the love of Christ, and to know this love that
surpasses knowledge.

Ephesians 3:17-19

A century ago, when American life was centered in its small towns, rather than the big megalopolises of the post-war era, the highlight of a year would be the arrival of the Big Top Circus to a town. When the cast of performers and their exotic animals pulled into the local train depot, the cars would be unloaded and the parade would begin. Right through the middle of town they would march to the site where the large tents were being erected on the outskirts. It was great advertising. The circus parade would whip up the excitement of all the citizens.

One day, as the circus parade went by, two boys in tattered overalls pressed themselves against a fence along the route to watch. Each had his eye in a knothole. As they gazed intently, the parade would flash by. "There's the elephant," would cry the one. "I think I see a tiger in a cage," the other one would yell out. "Here come the clowns," they would shout in unison as they caught a fleeting glimpse of the men in the big shoes with red noses. But it all whizzed by so quickly, and the boys could only observe the wonders of the parade from a very limited vantage point.

The Bible tells us that the great parade of eternity is passing us by, but we are only able to see small portions of it – like the boys peering through their knotholes. We simply cannot grasp the fullness of the wonders of the universe, let alone the vastness of the character of God. We catch only glimpses. That is what Paul is reminding us of in Ephesians 3. Though our sight is limited

> We are all so limited in our vision, seeing through the knothole only what is happening now, and from our own personal perspective. We can't view what has already passed by our vantage point, nor can we see what is yet to come. But suppose that somehow we were able to be lifted above the fence to a high vantage point, where we could see the whole parade at once, from beginning to end.

like a knothole, he is praying that we might be able to see and understand more of the infinite love of God.

He urges us to try to grasp the "width, length, height and depth" of this love. Some people, locked into their own limited perspectives, have wondered about God's love. Tragedy or suffering, hard times or times of boredom and depression, can block our eyes – temporarily covering over even the small knothole through which we try to grasp reality. But the great Apostle calls us to move those impediments away from our knotholes and see things properly. Most importantly, we need to understand the love of God.

God's love is WIDE: it is offered to everyone, no matter how unworthy they are. No one has any claim to it, nor any right to withhold it from another person. We are all equal before the Cross of Christ.

God's love is LONG: longer even than we can measure or count, beyond the moment that marks the end of our earthly lives, on into eternity without end. The Bible tells us repeatedly that our Father's love for us will never end, and that we are eternally secure in His embrace.

God's love is HIGH: it towers over the mundane and petty events of life, the way a skyscraper towers over the crowds rushing by on a city street. Just as the soaring heights of the Empire State Building beckon to the busy people on Fifth Avenue sidewalks to look up, so God's love summons us to look up from the things that distract and preoccupy us in our daily lives.

And God's love is also DEEP: it goes down into the depths of our souls. It reaches us when we have wandered far from the safe sheepfold of our Shepherd by seeking us out. No one can ever sin more than the grace of God can cover, if we will simply turn to Him and respond to His beckoning call.

We are all so limited in our vision, seeing through the knothole only what is happening now, and from our own personal perspective. We can't view what has already passed by our vantage point, nor can we see what is yet to come. But suppose that somehow we were able to be lifted above the fence to a high vantage point, where we could see the whole parade at once, from beginning to end. That is where God is. He is above the fence, where there is no past, present or future.

That is why the New Testament pleads with us to trust in the One who sees and knows all, and who has promised that His love is wider and longer, higher and deeper than anything else in this Universe. Though we can't see the whole parade of life, we can see Him who is above it. And we can place our complete faith and trust in Him.

Lord, in those times when our vision is restricted, and we can't see clearly what is happening or its ultimate purpose, we look to You for the perspective that only eternity can bring us. Help us to cling to the promises of the Word of God, and to believe firmly in Your love that has no limits. Help us to never panic or despair, but to trust You completely. Amen.

※

> He asked me, "Son of man, can these bones live?"
> I said, "O Sovereign LORD, you alone know."
>
> Ezekiel 37:3

There's no doubt that our generation suffers from moral uncertainty. There's searching on the part of youth for fun, but little real happiness. We're zealous for freedom, but we're weak in our worship of the Lord. We have everything, but possess nothing. We seek knowledge, but lack understanding. There's plenty of struggle upward, but we seem to continue to sink lower. We must have a rebirth of moral conviction and a regeneration of thousands of individuals if our generation is to be saved.

Since a renewal of spirit won't come to the world until it has first come to the church, we need to have our faith renewed. Before the world can be moved, we must renew the image of Christ in ourselves. It's sheer mockery for the church to call upon men and women to love their neighbors when the church has a lukewarm relationship with the Lord.

And the Lord said to me, "Son of Man can these bones live?" I said, "O Sovereign Lord, you alone know." Ezekiel will speak nothing in his own name. He doesn't guarantee one word of what he speaks by his own authority. The wondrous imagery of our Scripture lesson isn't the birth of his fancy; it's something which his soul's eye has seen. It was his business to deliver messages, not to make them. When he's incoherent, he makes no apology;

when we can't follow him, he can't help it. When he's apparently angry, he doesn't know it, he will only tell what he's seen and heard. He won't write a sentence, he won't study literary form. He knows nothing about taste, polish, style. He prays like a man who's sure he can have what he asks for. He's a thousand prophets in one, hence his peculiarities. His imagination so great, his command so authoritative, his threatening so appalling, his signs and tokens so bewildering, he knows nothing of what he's talking about.

Early in his life the prophet Ezekiel had been a witness to many a battlefield scene. He'd experienced many of the horrors and calamities of war. And this seems to have had quite an effect upon his ministry. His prophecies, more than any other prophet, are filled with terrific images and visions of dreadful things. In the lesson before us, he describes himself as set by God in the midst of a valley that was full of bones. It seemed as if he were positioned in the midst of some great battlefield where thousands had been slain and none left behind to bury them. The eagles had many a time gathered over the carcasses and no one scared them away. And the wolves of the mountains had eaten the flesh of these mighty men and drunk the blood of princes. The rains of heaven had bleached them and the hot sun had baked them bare.

Before the Lord gave to Ezekiel this vision of what he himself would do, he prepared him by first of all letting him see the true state of things. The question before us is this: Have we seen? What do we know? Before we lift up our voices and begin somewhat vaguely and vainly to talk, or even before we begin to talk of God's great power, before we begin to sing great hymns, psalms and praise songs, and say great prayers, let's go and see the real world. We won't have a mental or spiritual breakdown. It will break down our false confidence. Only the Lord God Almighty can save this world we live in.

No doubt there was an awful silence spread over this scene of desolation and death, but the voice of his heavenly guide breaks in upon his ear, "Ezekiel, can these bones live?" What a dumb question for God to ask! When Jesus said of the woman, "She's not dead, she's sleeping," they laughed. But here weren't bodies newly dead, but bones, bare, whitened bones. They weren't even skeletons. For bone was separated from its adjoining bone; and yet God asks, "Ezekiel, can these bones live?"

> You can be made alive by God's Spirit.
> It's not hopeless. Kneel beneath his
> cross and you will come alive.

Now, here we stand today and there's before us a vision just like that before Ezekiel. All the wretchedness, all the misery, all the helplessness – China, Iran, Iraq, Israel and Palestine; homelessness, AIDS, abortion as a form of birth control, murder, dishonesty, child abuse, wife abuse, alcohol, drugs – a mass of bones. Now before we do anything listen – listen; look – look; preacher, elder, Sunday school teacher, Bible teacher, youth leader, choir member, usher, member of this church – for God speaks. Yes, things are dark, dismal, desperate, depressing. Can these bones live?

Two answers. One is overly enthusiastic – "Yes!" I think I've heard that before. It doesn't impress me. It somewhat depresses me. And then there's an over despairing "No." It's hopeless. Death reigns. Hell is triumphant. Christianity has seen its day. It's hopeless. Neither answer is right, neither the over enthusiastic, nor the over despondent. Ezekiel was a smart, sharp man with a burning heart and as concerned as any of us and the most he could say is good enough for us. It was neither the over-enthusiastic "Hallelujah, praise God!" nor the over-despondent, "No way." It was what each one of us feels when we really come face to face with dry bones. "Can these bones live?" Looking at the bones I can't say yes, but looking at my questioner, I dare not say no. Stand there between God and the devil, heaven and hell. Stand in the middle; feel, see, and understand the situation. This is all God asks of us. He doesn't want our cheap God-talk answers. Don't become despondent, don't despair. "Can these bones live?" Only the Sovereign Lord can answer that question. Ezekiel knew that and responded accordingly. If God puts his living spirit into them, they'll live.

Ezekiel stands in the middle of the field of dry bones and, against all sense and reason, with earth and hell laughing at him, prophesies as the Lord commands. These bones were dead, dry, spiritless, lifeless, without flesh, without ears to hear … and yet God says, "Prophesy upon these bones and say to them, 'Dry bones, hear the word of the Lord!'" And so he prophesied, and "breath entered them; they came to life and stood up on their feet – a vast army."

The breath of God converts an organization into an organism, a congregation into a communion of believers, a mob into an army for God. Perhaps you feel spiritually dead. You can be made alive by God's Spirit. It's not hopeless. Open your heart and soul to him today. Kneel beneath his cross and you will come alive.

Sovereign God, can these bones live? You know they can!
Help me in my disbelief. Give me belief. I trust you for new life,
Father. I pray these things in Jesus' name, Amen.

✳

> Brothers, I do not consider myself yet to
> have taken hold of it. But one thing I do:
> Forgetting what is behind and straining
> toward what is ahead, I press on toward the
> goal to win the prize for which God has
> called me heavenward in Christ Jesus.
>
> Philippians 3:13-14

I enjoy looking up and seeing the engine trail of a jet cutting a straight path across the sky homing in on some distant destination. A few years ago Phyllis and I took a trip to England. I was moved while I watched the ship QEII disengage from the dock in New York, slowly make its way out to the harbor's edge, and then swing about pointing its stately prow toward Southampton, England some 3,000 miles away. And I'm inspired when I see a woman or a man who moves through life as though she or he is going somewhere and knows where they're going.

We are pilgrims living in a vagabond world. Note the words of the Apostle Paul, "One thing I do: forgetting what is behind and straining toward what is ahead, I press on toward the goal to win the prize for which God has called me heavenward in Christ Jesus." And the words of our Lord when He said, "Enter through the narrow gate. For wide is the gate and broad is the road that leads to destruction, and many enter through it. But small is the gate and narrow the road that leads to life, and only a few find it." Here Jesus is talking the language of travel. He speaks of two roads and of the different places they lead. He's not issuing a new law by which life is to be governed. He's simply pointing to two roads that are already there and advising us which we should choose as we make the journey of life. Paul gives us a goal to reach and that is the high calling in Jesus Christ.

There's a difference between a pilgrim and a vagabond. The pilgrim knows where she's going or where she wants to go and she's forever trying. The vagabond is a wanderer whose direction is determined by convenience. He does what's easiest or most expedient or appealing at the time like a boy kicking a tin can – wherever it lands he goes. Life is like that for a lot of people. They aimlessly blunder into any given moment of experience. Smash through it at its weakest point and then go on in whatever direction seems easiest or most attractive. A pilgrim is a traveler going from somewhere to somewhere.

Abraham had been a wanderer, a nomad, but God called him and he became a pilgrim. The Discovery Channel had a program on the Puritans. They wandered about the country of England and then sought refuge in Holland. They spent a long time trying to do what was easiest for them. But then they made a decision they would travel to the wilderness of North America and build a new home for religious freedom in the world. One hundred two of them boarded a little ship called the *Mayflower* and these homeless wanderers pointed that little vessel toward a new home across the sea. William Bradford, for 30 years the governor of their colony at Plymouth, wrote in his *History of Plymouth Plantation* concerning their leave-taking for America these words: "They knew they were pilgrims." No longer were those people wanderers or refugees, they were pilgrims. Now they moved with a purpose. They'd heard the call of freedom and they resolved to pursue it to the very death, and they did.

Most of our world is pretty much the vagabond kind. This isn't a new development in our day. Too many folk are pragmatists; the philosophy of living which says if it works it's okay. One of the most tragic troubles of the pragmatist is that he's myopic, nearsighted. He isn't looking far enough ahead; he doesn't have a long range view. He isn't really going anywhere. He's just kicking a can. He's determining his values and taking his directions from the illumination of the moment rather than the millennium. When we entrusted our lives to the Captain of the QEII, we wanted him to steer by a star and not by the contour of the next wave. If you fly in a 747 to Israel you want your pilot to be tuned in on the homing beam. You don't want her to fly by the signs she sees in the clouds and the winds.

But this is the way much of the world moves in the moral and spiritual and intellectual sense. And my friends, pilgrim living doesn't come easy in a vagabond world. Our temptation is to accommodate to what is around us. If our compass is to guide us well, its needle should be pointed to the distant pole. But too often it's deflected by local magnets. We must not be so weak as to permit whatever is nearest us at the moment to set the moral tone of our lives. Paul wrote, "Do not be conformed to this world." Phillips translates it, "Do not let the world squeeze you into its own mold." There's no way of living that is half as thrilling or adventurous as pilgrims living in a vagabond world to hear the beat of a different drummer. To see the glimmer in the distance, to hear a call from afar, or as Emerson put it, "to hitch your wagon to a star." There is no better quest than the one Paul spoke of when he said, "Seek what is above." Although we may never reach all the summits we aspire to, the pilgrimage has rewards of its own. In a drama the question is asked, "Have you reached the heights?" And the answer given is this, "No, but I saw them once and they're there all right."

In our world we have many voices seeking to guide us. They are confusing. Loud voices in one breath are heard speaking of all kinds of new moralities, psychic internal discoveries. Others assert the "rights of man" and the irrelevancy of God. More and more the individual person is the product of universal man and the black and white issues or moral caliber and quality are tending to disappear into a dreary shade of leaden gray. The fact is that somewhere between our vast systems and our little devices is a guiding star; that star is Jesus. Let us focus our attention on him. He is our prize.

And so Father, I confess that I have been influenced by other voices and have neglected yours. I have set my mind on the prize of knowing you and following your Son Jesus. My life does matter. Thank you for loving me and sending me into the world to live a life that shows others the good news of knowing Jesus Christ as Savior and Lord. Amen.

✺

Woe to those who call evil good and good evil,
who put darkness for light and light for darkness.

Isaiah 5:20

Humanity has always been dexterous at confusing evil with good, and this is exactly the mistake Isaiah is warning us about. All the way back in the Garden, Adam and Eve tried to re-label their blatant sin as a virtue: "It looks so good to eat, and if we do so we'll become like God." This is how we delude ourselves into "calling evil good and good evil." It's so common all around us today. A contemporary philosopher spoke for the spirit of our times when he wrote, "A wrong deed can be considered to be right if a majority of the people at any time think that it is not wrong."

But in spite of the constant changes and the moral confusion in our society, God and His Word have never and will never change. God has put a conscience within all of us to remind us of these unchanging moral rights and wrongs. To ignore its whispers, we humans resort to rationalization. And rationalization is not new. Jesus described, in the parable of the Pharisee and the Tax Collector in Luke 18, a man who was a master of rationalization: "I thank thee, Lord, that I am not as other men are." But Christ exposed the Pharisee for what he was: a hypocrite, a phony and a rationalizer.

The first step to avoiding the mistake of the Pharisee, and the disastrous error Isaiah warns us about, is to face the truth of ourselves. We all are prone to do wrong and need God's grace. The Tax Collector in the parable started here: "God, be merciful to me, a sinner." That is the starting point to becoming a moral person: not trying to obey a harsh ethical code, but receiving the grace of God through Christ and entering into a personal relationship with Him. We can openly admit our sins and wrongs, without trying to rationalize them or justify them or pretend that "evil is good and good evil."

> Perhaps today, or tomorrow, an opportunity will come to you to speak up for truth. It may be in a business situation, or a social context, or even in your marriage or your home. May God grant you the humility and the courage to do so and to not give in to the temptation to moral laryngitis.

And once we are on this path of humility and discipleship, we must learn how to avoid "moral laryngitis." This is the safe path that many are tempted to take. It means keeping silent, losing our voice, when we see things that are wrong. We all feel the pressure, in various situations and social settings, to lose our voice and have moral laryngitis. We are all tempted to say nothing when wrong is being done and our society approves of it. But the Word of God calls us to find our voice through faith and speak out, rather than losing our voice through fear.

How grateful we all must be that faithful people through the centuries have not given in to moral laryngitis. America exists as "the land of the free and the home of the brave" only because bold men and women centuries ago cared enough about human rights and dignity and justice to not keep silent in the face of tyranny. It was not the fearful and timid who made our country, but those who had the courage to find their voice and proclaim the truth. The pages of Scripture are full of similar people, men and women who by God's grace spoke clearly of the right and the truth even when it was not popular or convenient to do so. We thrill at the stories of Moses and Elijah and Daniel and Peter and Paul, who would not pretend that evil was good.

Perhaps today, or tomorrow, an opportunity will come to you to speak up for truth. It may be in a business situation, or a social context, or even in your marriage or your home. May God grant you the humility and the courage to do so and to not give in to the temptation to moral laryngitis.

Lord, I know that I am not perfect. But I will not try to justify my sins or rationalize them. I will confess them to you, and receive your mercy. And then I will seek to humbly be your mouthpiece in my portion of your world. Help me to be faithful to you in all I do and say. Amen.

※

"A new command I give you:
Love one another. As I have loved you,
so you must love one another."

John 13:34

I believe in the new birth experience. When the Holy Spirit enters
a person's heart and opens the understanding to God's truth
in Jesus Christ as Savior, one is born again and conversion
follows.

One of the dead giveaways of the Pharisaism of some self-
labeled "born again" Christians is the fact that they haven't been
freed from the law. The most casual reader of the New Testament
would find that this is the great emphasis of the graciousness of
our Christian faith; the true disciple of our Lord Jesus Christ is
freed from the binding senseless bondage of the law.

The ironic tragedy of the phony, counterfeit, contemporary,
born again Christian is that his new birth is most often evidenced
by his greater bondage under the law. The real heartbreaking
tragedy is that many of these well-meaning people seek to give
witness to their new birth by the restrictions that they impose
upon themselves and further by their oft-repeated contention
that anyone who doesn't follow these restrictions can't truly term
himself or herself a born again Christian. These restrictions are
usually in the area of personal pietism – the "touch not, taste not,
handle not" type of petty moralism.

Every year our national congress, our state legislatures, our county commissions, our city councils spend more and more time concocting more and more laws. And yet with an estimated 35-36 million laws on our statute books our lawlessness as a nation increases at the rate of five times that of our population. It's no wonder, then, that I want to heave every time I hear a fellow citizen make the remark, "There ought to be a law!" I want to shout back, "There already is a law." Now it is true that we live in a world that's sick with hatred and yet that hatred is an individual illness. Cities can't hate. Nations can't hate. Political ideologies or parties can't hate. The world is sick with hatred because individual human beings in the world are sick with hatred. That we see on every side. We see hatred in our very homes. We see families torn and mutilated by it. I'm sometimes interested to hear husbands and wives comment that they just don't understand why there isn't peace in the world. Why can't nations work through their differences peacefully? And I want to comment, "Since you can't do it in your marriage you ought to be able to understand the world's dilemma." Do you have any idea what a devastating experience it is for a pastor to again and again, week after week, be confronted with husbands and wives who share the same house, who sleep together in the same bed, who together have produced the same children, and yet literally hate each other?

Recently the husband of a divorced couple was telling me about how he and his wife send their children back and forth. He said, rather proudly, "You know when I have them I spoil them rotten. I give them everything they want. I let them do anything they want to do so that when they go back to her it drives her nuts because she can't control them." That takes a lot of hatred of both his ex-wife and his children to do something like that, doesn't it?

What's the answer to hatred? Well, certainly not diplomacy, not anti-defamation, not racial tolerance, not social engineering, not education, which we so often hear. We're brilliant haters; the world is full of clever devils. Then what's the answer? The word is love. Now, wait a minute. Before you close your ears and say you've heard this sermon before, because you've heard a sermon on love, maybe you aren't thinking of the same thing that I'm thinking about when I use the word "love."

> It doesn't ask you to decide whether that person is worthy of your love or whether he's ready for your love or whether he'll accept your love or whether he'll appreciate your love.

Those of you who are interested in preserving the law, in establishing the law, do you want another law? Well, this is the law! Strangely enough, you know, it doesn't have anything to do with not lying, or not stealing, or not engaging in illicit sex, or not drinking, or not murdering. The law of Christ doesn't have anything to do with not doing anything. The law is love and love is the law. "Love one another as I have loved you." Essentially the love of which Christ speaks is a life outgoing in sacrifice, outgoing to God, outgoing to our fellow human beings.

Booker T. Washington, the great black leader, understood. He said, "I resolve that I shall never allow any man to narrow or degrade my soul by making me hate him." You see, he knew that hate doesn't destroy the hated. It destroys the hater. The world is hungry for love. It's the love of God in Jesus Christ.

There's no order without law, and here's the law. The fulfilling of the whole law. "I command you to love one another even as

I have loved you." And that means you, and you, you and me. And you know, it's unqualified, it means to love all with whom you have contact. It doesn't ask you to decide whether that person is worthy of your love or whether he's ready for your love or whether he'll accept your love or whether he'll appreciate your love. The command is simple, "Love him." And how we need that law in the world today, practiced by born again Christians.

Loving Father, I thank you for loving me. That truth set me free. I know that the world will change one person at a time through love ... your love. May I love as you love me today, so that someone may see Jesus, know they are loved and make him their Savior and Lord. I want to fulfill the law of Jesus Christ.
In Jesus' name I pray, Amen.

※

We are hard pressed on every side, but not crushed;
perplexed, but not in despair;
persecuted, but not abandoned;
struck down, but not destroyed.
We always carry around in our body the death of
Jesus, so that the life of Jesus may also be
revealed in our body.

2 Corinthians 4:8-10

Sometimes you just know it's going to be a bad day. The comedian wisecracks about his bad days: "I called the suicide prevention line and they put me on hold. My horn got stuck behind a gang of Hell's Angels. The secretary buzzed to say that a *60 Minutes* film crew was waiting at the reception desk." One day on an airline flight from New York to San Francisco the pilot interrupted the movie to announce in reassuring tones, "Folks, those of you on the right side of the aircraft will notice that one of our engines is on fire, but don't worry. We can still fly." A few minutes later he came back on the intercom with the same reassuring voice: "Folks, one of our left engines has now stopped, but don't worry. We can still fly." A few minutes later a third engine died. The pilot suddenly emerged from the cockpit with a parachute on his back, opened the door, and said with his reassuring voice just before he jumped, "Don't worry, folks. I'm going for help." That's when you know you're having a bad day: when the pilot jumps!

The Apostle Paul knew what it was like to have bad days. He had many of them: imprisonments, beatings, shipwrecks, opposition. But he knew that his Pilot would never bail out. That's why he could write the confident words in today's scripture text. Paul was clearly one of those rare people who are never under their circumstances. It's common, when we're asked "How are you doing?" to reply "All right, under the circumstances." But Paul never stayed under his circumstances. He knew how to get above them.

> It's why we are drawn so much to the Cross. It was a symbol of shame, but it was transformed by grace into a means of salvation. Through that Cross we can do more than cope. We can conquer through His power at work in our lives.

What was his secret? Paul knew the transcendent power of God in his own life. Christ lived within him, and therefore nothing on the outside was strong enough to crush him. By faith he not only coped, he conquered. And so can we.

The opening line of Scott Peck's helpful book *The Road Less Traveled* is simply this: "Life is hard." He's right. The people who have made the most significant contributions to our world have been the ones who didn't shirk from this truth but confronted it head-on. They not only coped, they conquered.

Are you familiar with Wedgewood pottery? It's some of the world's finest. Did you know that Josiah Wedgewood was forced to leave school and go to work when he was only nine, and that at thirteen he was stricken with smallpox that crippled him for life? Nothing came easily for Josiah. But nothing could defeat him. And today the fruits of his labor are renowned worldwide for their consistent beauty.

Paul discovered that, by the grace of God, opposition often presented him with opportunity. Whenever he was delayed in his journeys, or sent on a detour, he took the opportunity to share the love of Christ with all he met. When he found himself stuck in prison, he took those opportunities to write the immortal words we find in our New Testament. Paul was convinced that wherever he was at any moment was where the Lord wanted him to be.

When I lived in New England, I always marveled at the way trees could grow in the narrowest stony crevices and most improbable places. Even on the rocky, windswept coastline of Gloucester on eastern Cape Ann we saw life sprouting up and hanging on. That's what faith in Christ is like: it grows and flourishes even in hostile situations and adverse conditions.

It's why we are drawn so much to the Cross. It was a symbol of shame, but it was transformed by grace into a means of salvation. Through that Cross we can do more than cope. We can conquer through His power at work in our lives.

Lord Jesus, you alone are the source of all the strength I need to cope with the hard times and challenges I face. Thank you that you are with me, that you never give up on me, and that by faith I can learn to conquer. Amen.

☀

This is what the LORD says:
"Cursed is the one who trusts in man,
who depends on flesh for his strength
and whose heart turns away from the LORD."

Jeremiah 17:5

A t times I say I trust God and yet a good part of the time I behave like mankind is more to be trusted. I trust man because I can see him. God I don't see, at least with the physical eye, and that counts a lot. We plug our ears to the words from the Prophet Jeremiah, that old pessimistic cry baby, when he said, "The Lord says, 'I will condemn the person who turns away from me and puts his trust in man, in the strength of mortal man.'"

Do you recall Mark Twain's *The Great Catastrophe*? Before he got to the last chapter he'd worked all of the characters into such a predicament that no matter what they did they'd be destroyed. He concluded the story, "These people are in such a fix that I can't get them out. Anyone who thinks he can is welcome to try." It's a picture of our world isn't it? We work ourselves into such predicaments in our marriages, relationships, business involvements.

I've been wishing that we could have a moratorium for two years – no one saying anything that would cause a crisis, a time when we stopped hurting one another and learning to enjoy each other. Would you like to try that for two years? How about for one week? Say for the next week I'm not going to say a word that will cause a crisis or hurt another person. This world seems to be an insoluble puzzle, an equation with no solution, a host of difficult questions and precious few answers. One philosopher put it this way: "No exit, no way out, too many people, too little space, too many births, too few deaths, no exit, too many mouths to feed, too little food, famine, starvation, malnutrition, inevitable, no exit, too many inequalities, too many injustices, too much hatred, too many divisions, no exit, too much war, too little peace, too much armament, no exit, too much time, too much lawlessness, too much immorality, no exit, too much wealth, too much debt, too much inflation, too much taxation, no exit, too little water, too much pollution, too little air, too much filth, no exit, too much to be done, too few willing to work, no exit, no exit, no way out!"

In times of peace the Christian faith is okay, but if things change somewhere in the world, give me a bomb and we'll talk about winning the world for Christ after we blow them off the map. "The Lord says I will condemn the person who turns away from me and puts his trust in man, in the strength of mortal man." Or, "It's alright to talk about being honest and obeying the commandments and I really try to do that in my home and I would like to be a Christian in my business dealings, but Frank, today business is tough and Christianity won't work in business if you want to be successful. It's a cold, cruel world outside your stained-glass ghetto, Frank. Your Christianity is a crutch, Frank. I'm not against Christianity, the Lord knows, I need God and I need this church if for nothing else as a refuge."

Have you ever thought about the danger of worshipping in this Sanctuary? I may be prejudiced, but I believe this Sanctuary to be a beautiful place. I'm very comfortable preaching from this pulpit. Most people entering this Sanctuary will automatically feel the lift that it gives. Our eyes are lifted to the Bible and the cross on the communion table and then to the cross and outstanding stained-glass window. This whole place produces an atmosphere of reverence. We feel that this is a place set apart from the world. And we need that, up to a point, and therein lay the danger. We all need a sanctuary in life, especially in a world and society torn by so much strife, trials and tensions. We all need a place to run to, a place of spiritual renewal, and a place to gain strength. We need that, but therein also lay the danger, the danger that our Christian life will become, in the end, an attempt to escape from life.

> Let's remember this, the Lord was and is a realist. The Christian gospel is for real. It doesn't reject the world and life in the flesh, it redeems the flesh.

What do I mean by that? Our spiritual life becomes so detached from the rest of our existence that we forget that while the church isn't of the world, the church certainly is in the world. And then we begin to look at Christianity as a beautiful ideal, our faith becomes effervescent, an elusive something that floats around somewhere up in the clouds. At that point Christianity is corrupted. We have detached it from life. We have emasculated it of its power and its reality.

The great danger of Christianity today is that it will become so idealized that it's no longer real. There's nothing to it. It becomes about as real as a kiss over the telephone. Let's remember this, the Lord was and is a realist. The Christian gospel is for real. It doesn't reject the world and life in the flesh, it redeems the flesh. Jesus was the divine Son of God in the flesh, but he had dirt under his fingernails and dirt between his toes, because he walked the roadways of life in this world with us. In the incarnation of Christ, the spirit and the flesh were joined together.

Christianity makes history significant. The kingdom of God has come to earth and the movement of history is the movement of the world toward the realization of that kingdom. And so the upward strivings of science and medicine and the arts are of vital importance to Christianity. The human mind and its talents and creativity are not despised, they're dedicated. The Word was made flesh, dwelling among us. Jesus cut to the very root of murder, which is anger. He cut to the root of adultery, which is the lustful glance or attitude. Yes, our Lord was for real and he wants us to be for real, too.

Is Christianity real and practical? Yes, Christianity is for real. Some of you were alcoholics – in Christ now you're sober; gossipers – in Christ you watch your tongue; adulterers – in Christ now you are pure. Some of you were dishonest – in Christ you are now known as men and women of truth.

Almighty God, you are alive. You made me alive. Keep me focused on the truth of the gospel that the good news is of grace, not law. But may I not cheapen grace, by ignoring the true root of sin. Give me courage to confess and repent. For I pray these things in Jesus' name, Amen.

※

The Spirit helps us in our weakness.
We do not know what we ought to pray for,
but the Spirit Himself intercedes for us
with groans that words cannot express.

Romans 8:26

Loneliness is epidemic, even in a world crowded with more than 6 million people. How can it be so that I could be lonely in the midst of people? Yet it's true ... true for single and married, young and old, of every race and nation. As one woman lamented to an advice column, "I live on an island, my husband lives on an island, and neither of us knows how to swim." The folk song of the '60's describes the prototypical modern person: "He's a real nowhere man, sitting in his nowhere land, making all his nowhere plans for nobody." Recent studies, including a book by sociologist Robert Putnam called *Bowling Alone*, describe the pressures towards separation and anonymity that our busy lifestyles cause.

But it doesn't have to be this way. Marlene Patterson, in her book *Alive Now*, hints at the way out. "Today I have another lonely day, Lord. The one phone call I received was a wrong number. Was there someone that needed a call from me, Lord, and I forgot about them? My neighbors waved at me as we went about our separate tasks, but we had no real conversation. Should I have sought them out? I sit in church on Sunday in the same pew, but I don't really know the people around me ... Am I lonely because I'm afraid to risk reaching out to another?"

Love is the cure for the world's epidemic of loneliness. As the great psychiatrist Dr. Karl Menninger wrote, "Love is the medicine for the sickness of the world. We love or we perish." I think he's right. We need to both give and receive love with other fallible but precious human beings. And above all we need to experience, deep in our hearts and souls, the incomparable love of God.

> As much as we need connection with others to remove our loneliness, deep inside our greatest longing is always for intimacy with our Creator. He created us with this need. And when we let Him into our hearts, we experience Him communicating to our inner loneliness and assuring us that He is with us.

We all have a need for deeper and more intimate, meaningful relationships. The single most powerful tool for developing deep sharing and intimacy is by taking the risk of reaching out and opening up. The story of Corrie ten Boom, the Dutch Christian woman who survived the Nazi death camp, is unforgettable. When she found herself herded into such an inhumane place she was tempted to sulk, to feel self-pity, to pull herself inward in self-imposed isolation, and to quit caring about anything and anyone. Yet something in her would not allow that. The Lord within her prompted her to serve the others around her and care more about them than herself. And in that cheerless, seemingly-hopeless camp abundant life broke out!

Our human nature cries out to be in fellowship with others. All the way back at the beginning, Genesis records that God's primary purpose in creating Eve for Adam was simply that Adam was lonely and needed companionship, a helpmate. "It is not good for the man to be alone" – that is the first thing in the creative process that was divinely declared to be anything other than good. The old Swedish proverb says "A shared joy is doubled; a shared sorrow is half a sorrow."

As much as we need connection with others to remove our loneliness, deep inside our greatest longing is always for intimacy with our Creator. He created us with this need. And when we let Him into our hearts, we experience Him communicating to our inner loneliness and assuring us that He is with us. Our text in Romans 8 tells us that the Spirit of God is actually praying to the Father within us and for us. Dr. Paul Tournier tells of a conversation with a patient one day. "I don't know how to say my prayers; what should I do?" He replied, "Just talk with God as you're talking with me, and even more simply. He understands your thoughts before you even form your words." Such an intimacy we can have with the Father through the Son by the infilling of the Spirit. We are never truly alone, for He is with us and within us!

Heavenly Father, at times I feel alone and separated from everyone. In those times of loneliness, help me to reach out to others with love for them. And help me to remember the promise of Scripture that I am never truly alone, and that you are always with me. Amen.

✸

"Though my father and mother forsake me,
the LORD will receive me."

Psalm 27:10

What do we do when our loved ones let us down? What do we do when we have been disappointed in someone we had trusted or rejected by someone we love, or hurt very deeply by someone who is very dear to us? What do we do? Here's a woman who gives the best years of her life to her husband. Then one day he walks away and leaves behind 20 good years and that is the end of that. It really hurts. Here are a mother and father who give their love and in love give everything to their daughter. But the day comes when she turns her back on them and on everything they hold dear; just as the Prodigal Son did to his father. One person said when this was happening to him, "When they're little they step on your toes. When they're big, they step on your heart. It really hurts." Here's a man who has a close friend whom he trusts and idolizes and with whom he shares some of his deepest thoughts. Then one day he discovers that he who seemed to be a friend was no friend at all and that all the while his friend had been laughing at him and working against him behind his back. It really hurts. Here is a young woman who grew up being loved very much by her parents but the day comes when she sees that there were always "strings attached" to that love. It really hurts.

In one way or another most of us have known how we feel

when our loved ones let us down. We have discovered that the people who can really hurt us, hurt us the most, are the people we have loved and trusted. It is those we love and trust who can hurt us most deeply. It's interesting how often we see this in the Bible and especially in the Book of Psalms. Many of the Psalms were written by people who say that they are being oppressed by their enemies. False witnesses have risen against them, their adversaries surround them, their foes are telling lies about them, the wicked are plotting to destroy them and they turn to God to deliver them. But some of the most impassioned of these Psalms were written not by persons who are oppressed by their enemies, but by persons whose friends or loved ones have now turned against them, and it really hurts.

We go to Psalm 27 and first we hear the Psalmist crying out to God about his enemies. Note verses 2-3 and 11-12. But as the Psalmist talks to God, he speaks not only of his enemies, but also of his loved ones who now have let him down. With the kind of brutal and realistic honesty that we are sometimes surprised to find in the Bible, the Psalmist says, "My father and mother may abandon me, but the Lord will take care of me." My father and mother may abandon me, my husband or wife, my son or my daughter, my brother or my sister, my friend or my companion … What does our Christian faith have to say to us when that becomes our cry and "when our loved ones let us down" and it really hurts? I think of three messages which our faith speaks to us.

The first message is that this is just the kind of thing you have to expect in this life because we live in a world in which human nature is limited. The Bible teaches us that we are not perfect but that we are sinners "Whose love is like a morning cloud like the dew that goes early away." (Hosea 6:4) A lot of people don't realize this and are surprised when they hear someone talk this way. They have the rosy, sunshiny view that Christianity is mainly a matter of "believing in folks." "Expect the best from people and the best is what you'll get." That sounds good, but it doesn't always work out that way. And it isn't what is taught in the Bible. From beginning to end the Bible gives a much gloomier view of human nature and portrays human beings as basically sinners.

> When our loved ones let us down … and it really hurts … God never fails, and God never lets us down. We can take our hurt to the Lord in prayer and he understands, personally, when it really hurts.

The second message our faith speaks is that even though someone has let us down, that person is not only a sinner, but is also in Christ a child of God. So we will continue to love him, to be patient with her, to forgive and to work for the recovery of the person he or she used to be. In all honesty we have to admit that this aspect is not always found in the Old Testament. Too often when the Psalmist was complaining to God that his enemies were oppressing him he wasn't asking God to forgive them, he was asking God to punish them. But you come to the New Testament and you find Jesus saying things like, "You have heard that it was said, 'You shall love your neighbor and hate your enemy.' But I say to you love your enemies and pray for those who persecute you."

Then there is the third message which our faith speaks to us. The love of other people may fail us and our efforts to love them may fail. But God's love never fails. When those we've trusted have been untrue, when those we've loved have turned their backs on us, we can rest ourselves in the assurance that God still loves us and that with a "love that will not let us go." God continues to reach out to us and to help us. No matter what disappointment we are going through, no matter how much we may have been hurt by someone we loved and trusted, God is with us to help us. Do you know why God is able to do this? God can do it because God knows just how we feel.

When our loved ones let us down … and it really hurts … God never fails, and God never lets us down. We can take our hurt to the Lord in prayer and he understands, personally, when it really hurts. So if my husband, or my wife, my son or my daughter, my brother or my sister, my friend or my companion lets me down or hurts me, the Lord will receive me. If my father and mother abandon me, the Lord will take care of me. When it really hurts, the Lord is always there. "Though my father and mother forsake me, the Lord will receive me."

Almighty God, you never fail those whom you have claimed as your own. May I reaffirm that truth today. I am a follower of Jesus and know that I have been called by him. To God be the glory as I learn by whom and through whom I am always loved.
In Jesus' name, Amen.

✳

I know what it is to be in need,
and I know what it is to have plenty.
I have learned the secret of being content
in any and every situation.

Philippians 4:12

There's something tremendously significant about people who can adapt themselves to the inevitabilities that life brings. There is so much dissatisfaction in our culture now. You know that a person is living a victorious Christian life when he or she accepts their situation, after making a real effort to change it. The acceptance of the inevitable: it's a mark of God's grace. Unfortunately, so many people haven't accepted the grace of being happy with what they have.

When Paul wrote the words of our text, he was in a Roman prison cell. If there was ever a situation that would seem worthy of being dissatisfied and miserable, surely this was it. Yet we hear not a word of complaint from the Apostle.

In the days of the protest movement called "the Scottish Covenant," Presbyterian Pastor Samuel Rutherford was removed from his prosperous parish of Anworth and imprisoned by the government in the cold gray desolation of the Aberdeen city jail. He maintained a steady stream of correspondence to his parishioners, encouraging and comforting them. He closed those letters with a remarkable sign-off: he did not write, "from my dreary prison cell in Aberdeen." Instead, Rutherford would close his letters with the words "from my Lord's Palace in Aberdeen." He, and Paul, believed that a dungeon could be every bit as glorious a home with God as a king's residence. That's what faith does: it transforms any situation of life into the Lord's presence.

Some of us allow ourselves to become discouraged too easily. We conclude that we're in the wrong place geographically, or socially, or economically, or vocationally, or relationally. The core problem is not our circumstance. The problem is that we have not properly adjusted our inner spiritual thermostat.

My pastor's study, in a church I served in New York state, had a problem in the winter time. The temperature in the office at times rose to an intolerable heat. And this was often on the coldest days, when the outside air temperature was in the single digits or lower. The problem was with the thermostat. Even after the furnace had lifted the room temperature to a comfortable level, the thermostat kept calling for more and more heat. It was stuck – and usually took a solid well-placed fist to get its attention and correct it! When a thermostat is stuck, the results can be very unpleasant. And that's what can happen inside our hearts when we get "stuck" on being discouraged and gloomy.

Notice carefully what our scripture is telling us. Paul is not just giving us a pep talk, telling us: "Don't worry, be happy." This is more than "positive thinking." The Apostle is revealing to us "the secret" of being content in all circumstances. What is that secret? It is yielding our self and our circumstances completely to the Lord. Can you honestly say to Him today, "I'm yours, Lord"? It's amazing what happens when you surrender your whole self to the Lord. You will find a contentment that runs deep within your soul. Your life will have new meaning.

I'm yours, Lord. I belong to you, all of me. I am in you and you are in me. Take me and use me as you will, whenever and wherever. And make me content with your perfect plan for me. Amen.

✻

"Lord, if it's you, Peter replied, "tell me to
come to you on the water."
"Come," he said.
Then Peter got down out of the boat, walked
on the water and came toward Jesus. But when
he saw the wind, he was afraid and, beginning to
sink, cried out, "Lord, save me!"
Immediately Jesus reached out his hand and
caught him. "You of little faith," he said, "why
did you doubt?"

Matthew 14:28-31

We have seen earlier the amazing experience that the
disciples had one stormy night, as their Lord
appeared to them walking towards their battered
boat across the waves. Mark tells us that they were initially
terrified – the fear every human has when we think we're
encountering a ghost or some other supernatural specter. But
their fear was replaced by calm and security as Jesus climbed
into their boat and the storm died down. For nearly twenty
centuries, believers have been comforted and reassured to know
that, whatever figurative storms may be "rocking" their boats, no
rolling sea or howling winds can keep our Lord from being with us
and giving us His peace.

But Matthew adds an interesting and fascinating twist to the
account found elsewhere in the Gospels (probably because the

author was actually there, an eyewitness). We learn about strong-willed Peter, and his attempt at water-walking. This story is a wonderful complement to the other accounts of Jesus calming storms and reassuring people who feel like they are passive victims of forces beyond their control. For in Matthew 14, we are invited to think about what we might do in the midst of our situation, what step of faith Jesus might summon us to take.

When Peter saw Jesus walking on the water he got so excited he had to make a request that he could do likewise. Jesus could have responded, "You dummy, don't ask for the impossible." It could have been a situation for a real "put down" for the impulsive Peter. The man who always seemed willing to leap before he looked could have been the object of ridicule by the other guys in the boat. But Jesus said, "Come." The words of Jesus come to me, "You have not because you ask not." But Jesus said, "Come." Many exhilarating opportunities have been missed because we have been afraid to step over the side of the boat into waters of new challenge.

Creativity is the rare combination of imagination and daring. Peter had it that day on the stormy sea. It is that first step that is so consequential. The invitation was given, "Come." Peter must be given credit for the courage to start moving. He got out of the boat. He was willing to risk appearing foolish in order to try something new, something he did not know would be "guaranteed or your money back in 30 days." Playing it safe would have snuffed out a miracle. Adventure to Peter was more important than his security blanket of the boat. I believe it is in the exercise of such daring faith that our potential may be realized.

Some Christians are "balcony types," those who endlessly discuss and debate the mystery of Christ – stewing over the pros and cons of belief and unbelief, the strengths and weaknesses of this theology and that theology – and never take a positive step of commitment to Christ. It is always easier to debate theology than it is to live it one inch in the right direction. Living one inch of the Christian life is worth more than a thousand miles of discussion about him. Don't sit in your boat or on the sand of the shoreline any longer. If you are getting a little weary of the dreariness of the shallows, launch out into the daring deep. You were not made for grubbing around in the sand, playing with little gadgets. You were created to ride the crest of the wave, for breathless encounters with God. When the next storm rolls in, ride it on the wings of an eagle.

Theodore Roosevelt said, "Far better it is to dare mighty things, to win glorious triumphs, even checkered by failure, than to take rank with those poor spirits who neither enjoy much nor suffer much because they live in the gray twilight that knows not victory or defeat." Peter's victory over fear was of very short duration. He encountered failure when he saw the wind, became afraid and began to sink.

One of the great dramatic sports events was when Babe Ruth pointed to the fence in a World Series game in Chicago and then drove the ball over it for a home run. After the game a reporter said to Babe Ruth, "Suppose you had missed and struck out?" A look of surprise came over the Babe's face and he said, "Why, I never thought of that." Now you and I know that life is not that simple. But we also are aware of the fact that nothing can dissipate our power faster than to think of failure. Then we shrink back from the possibilities that pulsate within us in partnership with God.

Peter's triumph was short, but so was his failure. He swallowed his pride and called, "Lord, save me!" He did not rationalize over his predicament but rather called for the rescuer.

And as the thief on the cross cried out to be remembered, Jesus immediately reached out to save. That is the type of God we have!

Jesus still stands on the stormy waves waiting to be called. His hand is there. Emerson said, "Some men live on the brink of mysteries into which they never enter and with their hand on the door latch they die outside." Don't let that happen to you. Call him. He is ready to reach down and put you on your feet again so you may walk tall in the presence of God.

God, I am calling out to you. I see your hand. I am coming to you. I am seeing you conquer my fear. Obedience is amazing. Thank you, Jesus, for loving me. You have such a wonderful purpose for my life. May I live faithfully in the steps of risk and obedience. In Jesus' name I pray, Amen.

✳

We live by faith, not by sight.

2 Corinthians 5:7

I s God with us, or is He not? People wonder that. And sometimes they jump to the wrong conclusion, based on the wrong
signs. One common mistake is to assume that if things are easy
for us, and we are prospering, and all is going well, then that must
be proof that God is with us. Smooth sailing doesn't always mean
the Lord is with us, or is pleased with us. Great men of scripture
wrestled with this seeming problem. Jeremiah asked, "Why does
the way of the wicked prosper? Why do all the faithless live at
ease?" Job, after a lifetime of faithfulness, was afflicted greatly –
while people of much inferior character to his seemed to prosper.
He asked, "Why do the wicked live on, growing old and increasing in power? Their homes are safe and free from fear; the rod of
God is not upon them; they spend their years in prosperity and go
down to the grave in peace." But just because fortune seems to
smile on you, that is no certain barometer for testing the presence
of God. His approval of us is not proven by outer circumstances.
Think of the examples of scripture (David committing adultery
with Bathsheba, Ahab defrauding Naboth, Judas betraying Jesus
with a kiss) who looked for awhile as if they were getting away
with sin and missing the consequences.

From the opposite perspective, difficulties do not mean
that God is absent from us. The people of Israel, after their
deliverance from Egypt, began to cross a dry and inhospitable

desert, and they cried out in their thirst that God had abandoned them. But of course He hadn't, and He summoned Moses to call forth water from the rock. Late one day Jesus directed His disciples to get into their boat and cross the Sea of Galilee. We might assume that, if they obey their Lord's command, all will be easy and prosper for them. But instead they encountered a violent, dangerous storm.

Our knee-jerk reaction to difficulties and troubles is often to doubt God's presence. When we have a flat tire or dead battery, when we lose a job, or break a bone, when our stocks decline, when a hurricane or flood comes our way, we wonder, *Why has God left me?* We must learn to trust God, even in the hard times. I find myself, in those times when the pastoral ministry is long and exhausting and difficult, needing to remember this truth. Of course serving the Lord is difficult. Nothing of true value in this life comes without effort. And that does not mean that God is absent, simply because things seem hard.

How do I know if God is with me? The guarantee of His PRESENCE is His PROMISE. And the scriptures are filled with just such a promise. Even if we can't see Him, Paul reminds us, "we live by faith, not by sight." Sometimes we simply have to trust in the dark.

It's a true story. A two-story house caught fire late one night. The hottest part of the flames separated the parents' bedroom from their only son's bedroom upstairs. Father and mother raced down the stairs, outside, and around to the place just below their son's bedroom. He had thrown open his window and was screaming in terror. The flames had him trapped, with no way to get to the stairwell.

The father assured his son that he was there, just below him, and then pleaded with him, "Jump, son. I'll catch you."

But the flames were so blazing that they were blinding, and the night outside was so dark, that the boy hesitated. "Daddy, I can't see you."

> Our knee-jerk reaction to difficulties and troubles is often to doubt God's presence. When we have a flat tire or dead battery, when we lose a job, or break a bone, when our stocks decline, when a hurricane or flood comes our way, we wonder, *Why has God left me?* We must learn to trust God, even in the hard times.

"Don't worry," the father replied. "Just jump. You don't need to see me, because I can see you."

That is what our Heavenly Father is saying to us. Though we may not be able to see Him, He always sees us and is ready to catch us.

Lord, help me to not be distracted by my outer circumstances into thinking that you are not with me. Help me to believe and trust, to rely on your promises, and to live by faith not sight. Amen.

✳

The light shines in the darkness,
and the darkness has not overcome it.

John 1:5

here is no way to speak of spiritual reality without some use of physical image. To portray a spiritual truth, we must choose a word picture that represents it. John the Gospel writer chose just such a word picture when he wrote in the Prologue to his life of Jesus the words of our text. What does he mean by "the light shines in the darkness"?

This is not talking about light in the cosmic sense – rays of a star shining into the blackness of outer space. No, he is speaking about something much closer and more intimate. John is referring to the darkness within us. This is an aspect of our personhood. If we are honest, we must face the reality of the moral and spiritual shadow-land of our minds and souls. It is to dispel this darkness, this inner shadow, that Christ comes to earth and seeks entry to every darkened heart. The very beginning of the Bible records that God created light ("Let there be light") and then created us ("Let us make man"). His purpose was that we, made "in His image," might dwell in His divine light. But through our disobedience we have all allowed darkness to enter our inner selves. The darkness within us conceals much that is beautiful and of precious worth. That is why God's purpose is to shine His light of grace: to drive the darkness away, that the beauty might shine forth.

The world that lies within us is the most important part of us. It is the place of our deepest hunger and longing, our highest aspirations and dreams, the world of struggle and quest, the world of feelings too deep for words. It's a wonderful world, this world within. It is wonderful in its potential to be bright and beautiful or dark and dismal. Deep within is the ultimate proving ground of all values. From within spring our highest virtues and our blackest vices.

A rose may be beautiful, but it brings no joy unless a human heart can receive it. A fortune in stocks and bonds can prove to be a misfortune unless it brings true contentment and satisfaction to the heart of its owner. The inner world is what matters. Into this world Christ wants to shine His light.

The wife and young son of a successful businessman were sitting on their porch one summer evening, looking at the stars. The mother spoke about heaven, and the little boy asked, "Will I go to heaven?"

"Yes," the mother replied.

"And will you go to heaven?"

She assured her son she would be there with him. The boy paused for awhile, and then said, "It's too bad Daddy won't be able to come to heaven."

"Why do you say that?" the mother asked.

"Oh, because he won't be able to get away from the office."

Actually, he will one day. When his time comes, the office won't be able to confine him, and that man will surely go to his eternal destiny. But that little boy revealed a great deal about his father. When we choose to limit our lives too much, we can shut out the light.

In 2 Timothy 1:10 we are told that Christ "has brought immortality to light through the gospel." We refer to things being "brought to light" when they are brought out of concealment and set in clear view. A fact is "brought to light" in court testimony. A news story is "brought to light" by the diligent reporting of a journalist. This is true with immortality and eternity: though for a time we may hide or obscure the eternal things by our darkness within, eventually all will become clear. The values that really matter will be exposed, along with our lives and our choices. But until we come to the end of our lifetimes, we have the opportunity to open up our dark places to the light of Christ.

Some things must always be essentially what they are. The pebble by the roadside is just a stone. Time and weather may change and erode it slightly, but it will always be just a stone. But that is not so with you and me. We are creatures of God's design and plan, and we have the potential to actually change. If we had the capacity to fall from God's grace, we also have the capacity to respond to that grace. If we could reach for the forbidden fruit, we can also reach for the hand of God. If we can sin, we can repent. If the prodigal son can wander from home, he can also return to the Father.

This is the most exciting and promising truth: that we can indeed change, by opening our lives to Christ. He wants to shine His bright light into our darkest places and brighten them.

Thank you, Lord Jesus, that you cared enough about me to come to this world, bringing your spiritual light. Help me this day to open my life to your light and allow you to shine in. Change me and mold me, Lord, that I might experience all you have for me. Amen.

✷

When we put bits into the mouths of horses
to make them obey us,
we can turn the whole animal.

James 3:3

T he wild horses we have to deal with are our instincts, the
untamed impulses of human nature. The Apostle James
had never heard of the psychologist William James, but he
knew something of the problems of the human heart. He had
never heard of Freud, but he knew the turbulence of desire. He had
never read a book by Carl Jung, but he knew about the conflicts in
the soul. "What is the cause of the fighting and quarreling that
goes on among you? Is it not to be found in the passions which
struggle for the mastery in your bodies?"

Wild horses, they're inside you. That's our problem and the
whole human problem in a nutshell: what to do with the wild
horses of human instinct? We come into the world with a powerful
set of impulses which, though back of all our sins, are
nevertheless the great driving force of life. We didn't create them.
They were wrought in our nature by the hand of him who made
man in his own image. Psychological research of the past 50
years confirms what the Bible has always taught us: that not only
in our bodies but in our natures, too, crouch these untamed
animal forces which, like wild horses, sometimes run amuck; and
that the great business of life is learning what to do with them.
What we are to do with the wild horses of human instinct?

The first answer is that of self-assertion. Let the wild horses run. Give free rein to your natural instincts. Do not inhibit or suppress a natural desire. The answer of self-assertion is to kill the riders and let the horses run. Obey your instincts.

The second answer is the extreme opposite of self-assertion: it is the answer of the way of self-negation. This answer holds that our primitive desires are so fierce that we must find a way to reduce them. The horses are wild, so we must tame them, take the fire and fight out of them and make them lie down and be still. The way of self-negation eliminates the horses.

The third answer is the way of Christ; self-fulfillment in the life offered in Jesus Christ. The answer of Jesus Christ is that these strong passions in our human nature must not be destroyed nor suppressed, but be put to use, pulled together in a supreme master-passion and consecrated to the Kingdom of God.

Faith in Jesus Christ is no opiate, putting the soul to sleep and taking the fight out of men. Look at the record. Look at the men he picked to follow him. It was public scandal that he spent so much of his time with rough and profane men, with sinners and disinherited earthy, half-heathen fellows, and that he chose his followers from among them. Jesus was genuinely attracted to the irreligious. They were stormy men, most of them, with turbulent passions that were often misdirected. Jesus did not fear enthusiasm or even fanaticism. He knew that torrents in men could be converted and harnessed, their power made to serve and to save.

The tongue, according to James, is at the heart of the discussion regarding the wild horses. James writes, "The tongue is a fire, a world of iniquity; so is the tongue among our members, that it defileth the whole body and setteth on fire the course of nature; and it is set on fire of hell." The tongue is a movable, muscular organ, found in most vertebrates, located on the floor of the mouth. The tongue in man is a very mobile structure and is an important accessory organ in such motor functions as speech, chewing and swallowing. It contains groups of specialized cells known as taste buds which are the special sense organs of taste and many nerve fibers which carry stimuli from the oral cavity to the central nervous system. The tongue informs individuals of changes which occur within the oral cavity. The central nervous system is kept informed by this membrane as to the consistency and state of salivation of food. Furthermore, the glands produce some of the saliva necessary for swallowing. The general appearance of the tongue has interested physicians for centuries, and the custom of having the patient protrude his tongue during an examination is not without meaning since certain changes in its appearance reflect disturbances in other organs and systems.

The Bible has much to say about the sins of the tongue. When a man gives way to anger and loses control of his tongue, he is committing sin. Every expression of anger, even the noblest form of indignation, is full of danger. Angry words never improved any situation. We are, for the most part, so utterly careless about letting ourselves grow angry we think it so impossible to help it. We take so little care to try to prevent it. The anger, wrath, bitterness, and scorn that are cherished in the heart come out in words of disdain and injury and in some cases go on to deeds of violence and mischief.

There are many sins of the tongue. Let me lift up three others. Take the sin of lying. The Bible puts lying alongside of murder and adultery. Lying is found in the realms of business and politics and social intercourse. I have heard many people boasting of their lying ability, especially in business. Some make a sincere effort not to tell a lie, but if circumstances prove embarrassing, many will not hesitate to lie their way out of a difficulty and consider it the lesser of two evils; the other being the consequences of admitting the truth.

Or take gossiping. There are many new things in the world, but gossiping is not one of them. A gossiper will only tell the truth when it will do more damage than a lie. Egypt cut off the ears and nose of those who offended. Athens first fined and then disenfranchised the gossiper. If I had the "gossip-bridle" franchise today I'd be a millionaire.

Or what about the sin of criticism; going around trying to see all the faults in others? Jesus said in Matthew, "Don't criticize and then you won't be criticized for others will treat you as you treat them." There are many Christians who would not dare do certain worldly things and yet they are filled with pride, gossiping, malice and sins of the spirit that are far more worldly and evil in God's sight than some of these outward things.

Pray to God for self-control. Self-control in speech is perhaps the greatest help. James writes, "Let every man be swift to hear and slow to speak."

Father, I have many wild horses that the tongue through expressed words run unbridled into reality. Forgive me for the ways words have damaged lives. May I tame the tongue, by your grace, in order for it to be used to advance the kingdom of God as opposed to thwart it. In Jesus' name I pray, Amen.

❋

> May the God of hope fill you with all joy and peace
> as you trust in him,
> so that you may overflow with hope
> by the power of the Holy Spirit.

Romans 15:13

Some Kentucky coal miners were trapped by a collapsing tunnel. The mining company scrambled to assemble a rescue team and reach the isolated men before their oxygen ran out. As the rescuers chopped their way closer and closer, they could hear tapping sounds on the other side of the rock wall. They listened carefully. One of the trapped miners had learned Morse code in his youth, and he was pecking out the desperate question, "Is there hope?" Thankfully for them, deliverance came before the air in their cave ran out. But their question could serve as a fitting one for all mankind. Many people, trapped in their own experiences, desperately are tapping out, in one code or another – by their thoughts or words or actions – the question, "Is there hope?"

The Apostle Paul makes it clear throughout his writings that the Christian faith is all about hope. It is what we offer uniquely to the world. It is what the Old Testament prophet Isaiah said the Messiah would do: "Prepare the way for the Lord; make straight in the wilderness a highway for our God. Every valley shall be raised up, every mountain and hill made low." The message to a seeking and hopeless world is what birthed the church. It is what believers through the centuries have clung to, even in the midst of seemingly hopeless life situations.

Some people are traveling a highway of depression, or discouragement, or even despair. For every one of us, the final stretch of life's road will be the highway of death. But along these hard roads, Jesus Christ meets us and walks beside us. And His presence gives us, as Romans 15 says, a "joy and peace as you trust in him." It turns our dark highway into a highway of hope.

But just as Christ's mission is to keep our hope alive and strong, the object of the devil in human hearts is to steal away our hope. The enemy of our soul tries to substitute false hope for the real thing, whispering to us that a bottle of alcohol or pain-killing pills will be our short-term solution. He tells us that an exotic vacation, a new car, a new house or a new spouse is what we need. All of these may bring pleasure for a season, but they are transient compared to the lasting hope that Jesus offers.

> We who also have the New Testament, with its revelation of the One who came in the flesh to reveal the full love of the Father, have even more confidence. Regardless of the circumstance in which we find ourselves, if we believe in the Word of God we must never give up hope. He pours it into our hearts, not just to fill us to the brim but even "overflowing."

Modern medicine confirms for us the necessity of hope. Doctors have told me that the presence or absence of hope in their patients makes all the difference – in their ability to endure treatments, surgeries or other medical procedures, and also in their mental health. People need hope to survive.

In the dark days of Nazi oppression in Germany during the Second World War, a few Jews were hiding, undetected, in the basement of Cologne Cathedral (protected from discovery for months by a few courageous Christians). On the wall of their basement hiding place they scratched out these words: "We believe in God, even though He is silent. We believe in the dawn, even though it is dark." Those Jews knew enough from the Old Testament to cling to their faith that God could be the source of hope. We who also have the New Testament, with its revelation of the One who came in the flesh to reveal the full love of the Father, have even more confidence. Regardless of the circumstance in which we find ourselves, if we believe in the Word of God we must never give up hope. He pours it into our hearts, not just to fill us to the brim but even "overflowing."

Jesus, at times my road through life seems difficult. At times I wonder if there is any hope in going on. Thank you for your assurance through the promises of scripture that you are always with me, and that you offer me a lasting hope that nothing can take away. Help me to cling tightly to that hope at all times. Amen.

✳

"But blessed is the man who trusts in the LORD, whose confidence is in him."

Jeremiah 17:7

The story is told of a farmer and his wife in the dusty panhandle of Texas. That is about as close to hell as I would care to get. They'd eked out a meager living for 30 years. One day an impeccably dressed man driving a fancy car came to their door. He told the farmer that he'd good reason to believe there was a reservoir of oil underneath his property. One member of my church in Kansas has such a well in the panhandle that yields him $900,000 a year. If the farmer would allow the gentleman the right to drill perhaps the farmer would become a wealthy man. The farmer stated emphatically he didn't want anyone messing up his property and asked the gentleman to leave. The next year about the same time the gentleman returned with his nice clothes and another fancy car. The oilman pleaded with the farmer and again the farmer said no. This same experience went on for the next eight years. During those eight years the farmer and his wife struggled to make ends meet. Nine years after the first visit from the oilman the farmer came down with a disease that put him in the hospital. When the gentleman arrived to plead his case for oil, he spoke to the farmer's wife. Reluctantly she gave permission to drill. Within a week huge oil rigs were beginning the process of drilling for oil. The first day nothing happened. The second day brought only disappointment and dust. But on the third day, right about noon, black bubbly liquid began to squirt up in the air. The oilman had found "black gold" and the farmer and his wife were instantly millionaires. They'd been sitting on a reservoir of wealth while they struggled to make a living.

A famous American author tells about meeting a young American traveler in the airport in Hong Kong. She was tensely occupying a chair next to his. When the tears began to drip from her chin, he imagined some lost love. But then she began to sob. She wasn't quite ready to go home she said. She'd run out of money. She'd spent two days waiting in the airport on standby with little to eat and too much pride to beg. Her plane was about to go and she'd lost her ticket. The author and a nice older couple from Chicago dried her tears. They offered to take her to lunch and to talk to the powers that be at the airlines about some remedy. She stood up to go with them, turned around to pick up her belongings and screamed. They thought something terrible had happened to her. But no, it was her ticket. She found her ticket. She'd been sitting on it for three hours.

What is it you're sitting on? In this grand world of opportunity do you have possibilities and potentials which are lying unused? The first point I wish to make is this: God's will for his children is to be successful. Now, someone is silently saying, "Hold on, Frank, is this that prosperity gospel I've been hearing so much about, where if you believe the right things and do the right things God is going to make you rich?" Not at all. Let's approach the question from the other side. Do you believe it's God's will for his children to live in squalor and poverty, ignorance and fear? Do you believe it is God's will for His children to live cold, bitter lives of defeat? None of us believe that. If that were true, why would Jeremiah have written, "Blessed is the man who trusts in the Lord?" Blessed means happy. It means contented, at peace with yourself. That's God's will for your life and mine. If we're not at peace with ourselves right now, it may be because we're sitting on some gift, some opportunity, some potential blessing to yourself and to the world.

> God has provided us means by which our dreams can be achieved.

It's not God's will that we should endure lives of quiet desperation as the poet expressed it. The Lord's will is for life abundant. God's will is that we have dreams and that we achieve those dreams. This isn't to say that sometimes our dreams don't have to be adjusted. They do. Former president Jimmy Carter dared to dream he could become President of the United States. He achieved that dream, but world events turned against him. Carter had to repair his dream and he did. He dedicated his time to helping the poor through Habitat for Humanity building low-cost housing. He and Rosalyn teach Sunday school and they've written six books since 1981. Rosalyn wrote, "If we have not achieved our early dreams, we must either find new ones or see what we can salvage from the old. There is clearly much left to be done and whatever else we are going to do we had better get on with it." Dare to dream. God's will for his children is to be successful.

God has provided us means by which our dreams can be achieved. The Lord didn't create us to wallow in despair and self-pity. I'm always amazed at how many bright, talented, energetic people thwart their dreams by self-defeating attitudes. They're doomed not by forces on the outside, but from within. In God's world there is a niche for every one of us. But many of us are sitting on our opportunities.

The secret is to trust in the Lord. "Blessed is the man who trusts in the Lord," writes Jeremiah. The crucial ingredient in achieving our dreams is confidence. Some people keep their dreams bottled up inside. Something holds them back. That something is fear. It takes a lot of courage to show your dream to someone else. They might laugh. They might not understand. Worse, they might take it out of the box and drop it and where would you get another one? Dreams are fragile. Some people in desperation give up on dreams. What is special about those who dream? They have the courage to go for it.

Where do you get the courage to reach for your dreams? For many of us it comes from our faith in the Lord. We believe that it's God's will that we live successful lives, however we might define success. We believe he has given us everything we need to achieve our dreams. All we have to do is trust him and venture out boldly to live the kind of lives he's called us to live. No more sitting on our tickets. No more sitting on our fortunes. No more sitting on our hands. No more sitting on our dreams. Follow your dreams by trusting in the Lord to supply your needs. Blessed are those who trust in the Lord.

God, you are the giver of dreams. You have made me in your image and given me the purpose of being a disciple of Jesus and making others disciples. I am fearfully and wonderfully made to live a dream which gets at your primary mission. Give me the courage today, God, to live the dream you have given me. In Jesus' name I pray, Amen.

✳

They all joined together constantly in prayer.

Acts 1:14

A man returned to a computer store the day after he had purchased the finest and most up-to-date product that store carried in its inventory. "I need some help with my computer," the man explained. "I can't get it to do what I want." The saleswoman, remembering the man from the day before, gushed to him, "Oh, sir, that computer can do everything. It's the top-of-the-line, the state-of-the-art." She went on describing the massive megahertz processor, the huge amount of RAM, the CD and DVD features, the 15 gigabyte hard drive, and the built-in Bose Surround Sound system. "That's all very impressive," the man affirmed. "I'm sure it will be great. But I can't figure out how to turn it on." Those who are not computer-savvy and who find themselves "technologically challenged" can relate to this poor guy's dilemma.

At a deeper level, this man's question is one that confronts us all. We have available to us far more knowledge than the ancients. We are blessed with so many creature comforts and amenities. But how do we turn the power on in our lives? We know from our scripture text for today where the power came from for the earliest Christians in the New Testament: their power came from prayer. After our Lord's ascension they gathered in the Upper Room in Jerusalem and were "constantly in prayer." And a few days later, on the great Day of Pentecost, the Holy Spirit flipped the switch. The power of God surged through them. Let's not fail to notice that it was constant, seeking and waiting prayer that unleashed the power.

Christians twenty centuries later likewise have found this secret of power for living. One who learned the secret was Eric Liddell, British Olympic champion, the subject of the Oscar-winning film *Chariots of Fire*, and a missionary in China in his later years. During the Second World War he was being held in a Japanese prison camp. His spiritual strength and inner joy kept all the rest of the prisoners from giving in to despair. One woman who survived the camp wrote of Eric Liddell's secret: each morning he would rise before anyone else and sit at a small table reading and praying. Starting out each morning by drawing on God's power enabled him to face whatever challenges came that day. People who accomplish great things for the Lord invariably have their lives plugged in to the power of God's love and mercy through prayer.

> Praying and prying: what an effective combination for all of us! Instead of the typical impulse of our human nature – which is that when we get in a tight spot we complain and cry – we should follow the teaching of God's Word to pray and pry. We should pray as if everything depends on God, and pry as if everything depends on us.

Prayer is not a meaningless ritual. Certainly some people abuse prayer in this way. And some non-Christian faiths practice repeated mindless chanting of holy words without any thought or meaning. But that is not New Testament prayer, and there is no power to be found in mere ritual.

Nor is prayer a substitute for our own hard work. God never intends for prayer to serve as a way for us to avoid our own responsibility. A lawyer named Charles Sinclair, in Coral Gables, Fla., was kidnapped by criminals and locked in his car trunk. As his assailants sped away to their hideout to hold him for ransom, he managed to escape. When the car slowed at a stoplight he popped open the trunk, crawled out and ran to safety. He had made his escape by using the tire iron inside the trunk to break open the lock and latch. He commented to reporters afterwards, "During those tense moments before my escape I was doing two things: first, I was praying with all my might; and second, I was prying like mad."

Praying and prying: what an effective combination for all of us! Instead of the typical impulse of our human nature – which is that when we get in a tight spot we complain and cry – we should follow the teaching of God's Word to pray and pry. We should pray as if everything depends on God, and pry as if everything depends on us.

The kind of prayer that brings power is a prayer that offers daily to the Lord our deepest concerns, trusting Him to help us deal with them. Such prayer brings power because it allows us to relax and focus on the things we need to do. Have you discovered how much power there is in prayer?

Lord, there are times when I feel such a lack of power in my life. But I learn in Scripture about ordinary people like me who have received your power. I want to experience that for myself today. Help me to pray in the right way, with the right spirit. Help me to do the best I can do, and also to trust you completely. Amen.

✳

This is the message you heard from the beginning:
We should love one another ... Do not be surprised,
my brothers, if the world hates you. We know that
we have passed from death to life, because we love
our brothers. Anyone who does not love remains
in death ... This is how we know what love is:
Jesus Christ laid down his life for us. And we ought
to lay down our lives for our brothers ... And this is
his command: to believe in the name of his Son,
Jesus Christ, and to love one another as he
commanded us.

I John 3:11-23

There is a certain indomitable quality found in the lives of
most human beings. Often it is a recessive trait, one not
too quickly or too easily seen. Perhaps a majority of us do
not even suspect its existence in ourselves, though we may see it
in someone else. It consists of a certain stamina, a certain spirit, a
certain strength. And it enables all who have it to venture, to
persevere, to face difficulty or danger or even death, and to
withstand them all with firmness and with resolution. This
indomitable quality found in the lives of most human beings, yes,
found in the lives of most of us, is called courage.

Almost always courage is something we think of in connection
with someone else, not ourselves. Yet it is there. For instance,
a squad of soldiers crouches in a bunker waiting for a signal to

move forward to engage the enemy. Suddenly there is a soft thunk as an enemy hand grenade lands right in the middle of the bunker. One private in the squad sees the grenade land. He is an ordinary soldier, half petrified with fear. And he has everything to live for. But in an instant he catapults himself on top of the grenade. It explodes, the private takes the full force of the explosion ripping into the soft parts of his body and he dies. As a result of his action, the other members of his squad, his buddies, remain alive and unhurt. He dies that they might live. Just a soldier, an ordinary guy, nothing special, he thought. But we call that man a hero. We call what he displayed extraordinary courage.

> But you know something? Often I think it is easier to lay down your life for someone else than it is to pick up your life for someone else. Courage is plenty difficult when it calls for the sacrifice of dying. But courage is even more difficult when it calls for the sacrifice of living.

That's the way it almost always is with heroes. They don't think they are heroes. They don't think there is anything spectacular about their behavior. But what they have, and what they exhibit, is that certain indomitable quality of human spirit known as courage. And when we think of courage, what we usually think of immediately is this raw risk-taking, death-defying bravery displayed on behalf of a very close friend, or sometimes even a total stranger in need. So, true courage, we would conclude, is the willingness to lay down your life for someone else in need.

That's rather extreme to be sure. But that's the way Scripture tells it. In the letter which we read today, the author emphasizes the necessity of Christian love. We experience Christian love, he explains, by experiencing the Christian Lord Jesus Christ. "This is how we know what love is: Jesus Christ laid down his life for us. And we ought to lay down our lives for our brothers. Dear children let us not love with words or tongue but with actions and in truth." That's the way it really is; that's the way it has to be. True courage is love in action. It is more than merely talking about how much and how deeply we love. It is more than merely expressing verbally to someone that we really love them. True courage is love which dares danger and defies death in order to truly serve a fellow human being. That's how we traditionally have thought of courage: something spectacular, something special, something found only in other people who are genuine heroes.

But you know something? Often I think it is easier to lay down your life for someone else than it is to pick up your life for someone else. Courage is plenty difficult when it calls for the sacrifice of dying. But courage is even more difficult when it calls for the sacrifice of living. Someone has said, "There are many people willing to die for their country, but too few who are willing to live for their country. There are many who are willing to die for their family, but too few who are willing to live for their family." So often we think of courage as one heroic act – a soldier throwing himself on a grenade, or an accountant dropping a baby from an upstairs window to safety. What we seldom fully realize is that courage takes a lot more guts when it consists of those little daily acts of heroism which usually go unnoticed and unpublicized.

Courage is that certain indomitable quality found in the lives of most people. It is related to love, closely related to love. It seeks to serve other people. Courage can be seen as a burst of heroic energy, a sudden dramatic action in which we lay down our lives, or at least risk our lives for someone else – stranger or friend. More important, however, is that quiet courage which seeks simply to live in loving service, even when the way seems painful, discouraging, distressful or lost. This quiet courage can make of even the most common, most ordinary life that which is truly noble in the sight of man and in the sight of God.

Father, I am asking for courage. May I not shrink in the face of conflict, challenge or persecution for the sake of the gospel. May I seize the moment to hold true to your Word and love my neighbor. Keep me faithful to you, oh God, for the sake of Jesus. It is in the strong name of Jesus Christ I pray, Amen.

✳

I do not understand what I do.
For what I want to do I do not do,
but what I hate I do.

Romans 7:15

We've all heard jokes about people who live in asylums, like the one about the three patients who were conversing one day. The first insisted that he was Napoleon. The second was doubtful. "How do you know you're Napoleon?" he asked. The first replied, "Because God told me." The third quickly answered, "I did not." We laugh, but we know it's not just behind the walls of padded cells where we find humans who have deluded themselves about who they really are.

The Bible bluntly confronts the contradictory nature of human beings. There is a part of all of us (our true self) that belongs to God, was created in His image, and longs to live out our true purpose in fellowship with Him. But very often our actual daily lives are distorted and twisted beyond recognition. Some other "self" takes control and directs our thoughts and actions. When we honestly face this inner contradiction, it can be quite frustrating and discouraging to us.

The old legend tells of the interchange between God and the Devil one day. God announces that He is going to limit the powers of the Devil, leaving him only one ability to use to torment people. "Which will you choose?" the Lord asks.

"That's easy," Satan replied. "Give me Discouragement. If only I can thoroughly discourage people, they will quit trying to follow you and will be mine forever."

Discouragement is truly a great weapon in the hands of the Evil One.

Our modern society seems to be cooperating with the Devil in his work of discouraging us. In an advice column, a woman described her visit to a prominent psychologist. "He told me I should stop going to church, because it always made me feel guilty. Instead I should just accept myself the way I am. Is that the right approach?" she asked the columnist. If she'd asked me, my answer would have been, "Certainly not!" Shutting off our conscience because it reminds us of our moral nature and convictions is no way to lasting happiness, according to God's Word.

The alternative is the way of struggle. Any positive change can come only through struggle. It is the struggle between the sinful nature and the godly nature within us that defines our lives as Christians. If we quit trying, we will never approach, even for a moment, the heights to which God has called us.

Again and again in my pastoral ministry I have seen Christian men and women – often in the midst of great crises or emergencies – display almost superhuman internal strength and courage and resolve. In fact, it *is* superhuman in a sense, because it comes to them through the Spirit of God working within them. And yet, their bold and faithful choices to follow the Lord allow them to be fully human and realize what they were created to be.

As long as we live we will be tugged in two opposite directions. Our lustful and greedy and foolish and proud and assertive self will compete with the self in us that desires above all to please our Heavenly Father.

I used to think that it was nonsense to believe we could "hate the sin but love the sinner." And then I realized that I had been doing that my entire life – to myself! I hate it when I fail to follow my conscience and my highest motives. Yet I love that part of me that is my true self, the me created by God. That's why I have learned to accept His forgiveness each day, and keep on trying anew.

Listen to these wise words of a man who might well be called the true Father of Psychology, because of his ground-breaking insights into our true nature. In analyzing himself critically and honestly he wrote, "I often find I have the will to do good, but not the power. And the evil things that I don't want to do are the things I end up doing. What a wretched person I am. Who will rescue me from this endless cycle? Thanks be to God through our Lord Jesus Christ, for He gives me the victory." Those are the words of St. Paul. Couldn't we all speak them about ourselves as Christians?

Woven into the seamless story of that classic parable of Jesus, The Prodigal Son, we find this profound insight. When the young son had squandered his inheritance and found himself in the lowest place imaginable for a high-born Jewish boy – slopping pigs in a pagan land – the text tells us, "Then he came to himself." He realized who he really was. "I am not a pig. I am a man. More than that, I am the son of my father. I will therefore return to him, and plead his mercy, and begin again to be my real self." This is what every Christian is called to do daily: to "come to ourselves," to receive our Father's forgiveness, and to begin afresh to live as our real selves, created to please Him.

Dear Father, I stray from you so often. I acknowledge to you my sins and wanderings. I want to come back to you this day, receiving your mercy, and beginning again. Help me to turn aside from those temptations and sins that would take me away from who I was created to be. Help me to live as my real self, to your glory. Amen.

✳

Who of you by worrying
can add a single hour to his life?

Matthew 6:27

One of the most frequent and nagging sins of Christians is worry. Though we say we believe in a God who is our Heavenly Father and who rules heaven and earth, we too often deny this fundamental truth by the way our minds become preoccupied with worries and fears about the future.

W.H. Auden called our modern times "The Age of Anxiety," and Albert Camus labeled the 20th century the "century of fear." Worry seems to be universal. Religious people worry and skeptics worry. Men worry and women worry, young people worry and "seasoned" people worry. Some of us worry about personal problems, others about community and world problems. The Bible reminds us that worry and anxiety have plagued mankind from the very beginning. Even with all our technology, our advancements in psychology, and our great wealth, the cancer of worry still plagues us.

A Christian soldier who went into Normandy on D-Day carried in his pocket the following words to help him combat the enemy of worry. "Of two things, one is certain: either I will be at the front, or I will be behind the lines. If I am at the front, of two things one is certain: either I will be exposed to danger, or I will be in a safe place. If I am exposed to danger, of two things one is certain: either I am wounded or I am not wounded. If I am wounded, of two things one is certain: either I will recover or I will die. If I recover, there is no need to worry. If I die, I can't worry in heaven. Either way, I do not need to worry!"

J. Arthur Rank, the famous English motion picture producer, had a rather unique approach. He knew that he was prone to worrying, and that it often crippled him. He came up with a unique way to conquer worry. He decided to do all his worrying on a certain day of the week and on no other. He set aside Wednesday for his worrying, and called it the Wednesday Worry Club. When a worry occurred to him on any other day of the week but Wednesday, he wrote it down and put it in a box. When he opened his box each Wednesday, he often found that those things he had been disturbed about had already taken care of themselves, one way or another. The rest he would think about for awhile and then lock them back in his box until seven days later. Perhaps some of us need to join the Wednesday Worry Club.

> Worry never gets us anywhere. It has never lifted a single load, it has never solved a single problem. Someone has wisely said, "Worry has never rubbed out a single wrinkle, but it has certainly rubbed in millions of them."

Cardiologists place worry as one of the leading causes of heart disease. The stress and anxiety it triggers can certainly be dangerous to body, mind and soul. This is why our Lord asked the pertinent question, "Who of you by worrying can add a single hour to his life?" Jesus is not telling us we should never think about the future. When He tells us "do not worry about the future," He doesn't mean that we are never allowed to look ahead. He is simply warning us about dwelling on apprehensive and fearful thoughts about tomorrow.

Worry never gets us anywhere. It has never lifted a single load, it has never solved a single problem. Someone has wisely said, "Worry has never rubbed out a single wrinkle, but it has certainly rubbed in millions of them."

The supreme antidote to the poison of worry is daily faith in God through His Son. We must learn to trust Him. If we spend the majority of our hours worrying, we are really saying to the Living God, "I don't believe in you."

Said the robin to the sparrow,
"I should really like to know
Why these anxious human beings
Rush about and worry so."
Said the sparrow to the robin,
"Friend, I think that it must be
That they have no heavenly Father,
Such as cares for you and me."

Gracious Father, you love us more than the birds of the air and the lilies of the field. You have proved to us how precious we are in your sight by sending your Son to be our Savior. Help us, Lord, not only to trust in you for our eternal salvation, but also to trust in your grace daily to overcome worry. Amen.

※

But I said, "Should a man like me run away?
Or should one like me go into the temple to
save his life? I will not go!"

Nehemiah 6:11a

A
s humanity's problems mount, many look to the biblical
faith with more desperation. The past 25 years have
been trying years for both church and society, causing
many to plead, if not outwardly then inwardly, "God, do
something." W.H. Auden, the poet, said, "If we really want to
live, we'd better start at once to try. If we don't, it doesn't matter,
but we'd better start to die." John R. Mott, that great Christian
statesman, once said, "The world is waiting for the witness of the
people called Christians." And I amend to say, "The United States
is waiting for the witness of the people called Presbyterians."

Unfortunately, a great deal of the vitality of American spiritual
life is not found in our so-called main-line denominations. A
number of years ago, ecclesiastical social activists confused
Christianity with the social gospel "democracy" and instead of
bringing in the kingdom of God as they promised they would,
their efforts gave rise to a massive muddle of confusion and
today we have the fruit of their labor. The conservative wing of
the church hasn't been without excuse. While we were busy
arguing whether Christ was coming before or after the tribulation,
the world around us was going to hell, spiritually and physically,
and no man really cared. These facts are crying for restatement,

particularly because the voice of many churches that should be raised in warning and appeal instead preach the obnoxious lie that somehow we will wake up in the morning and find that all is well.

You don't have to be a theologian to figure out that all is not well and it isn't getting better. The veracity of this as it applies to our own Presbyterian Church was graphically illustrated to me in a letter which I received from the late Don McClure, a former Presbyterian missionary in Africa. The letter was written 20 years ago, but so true even today. He wrote:

> The forces of secular change are not only gaining speed daily but the Church of Jesus Christ is slowly losing its impetus and is beginning to bank its fires and cut its budget for outreach throughout all of Africa. I believe this loss of vision and will to win Africa for Christ by our denomination is the result of several other losses which have gradually crept upon us and which have eroded away our spiritual strength. We have lost our faith in the power of the gospel to save souls. We have lost our confidence in the Word of God as the Living Word with power to cut through all racism, classism, colonialism, secularism, tribalism and just plain human depravity. We have lost the thrill of carrying out the command 'go ye into all the world and preach the gospel' and we have lost our belief in the Lord Jesus Christ that he can save to the uttermost. As a substitute for these losses we have become enamored of a social gospel and have become social activists. We have substituted cleaning up streets for cleaning up souls, building a man a house instead of building the kingdom of God in his heart, helping men start a business instead of teaching him the King's business of saving souls, training secretaries, doctors, lawyers, farmers with little concern about training them to be men and women of God. We

have become so mixed up in our spiritual priorities that we think just 'doing good' is good enough. It may be for government agencies, but it is not 'good enough' for the Church of Jesus Christ.

Facing this critical day in our church we ask the question of Nehemiah, "Should a man like me run away?" The old walls of Jerusalem were going up again. Nehemiah had managed somehow to arouse his despondent countrymen and, out of the rubbish and ruins, the walls were taking shape. All around were sinister enemies who wanted no strong Jerusalem and were doing everything short of violence to prevent it. They tried to laugh it off. But Nehemiah had his ears stuffed with cotton and couldn't hear them. The ugly rumor got started that Nehemiah might have an unfortunate accident. And then he said, "Should a man like me run away?" There's a good picture to hang in the front room of your mind today and tomorrow and the next day, a man standing up to life, staying with it when the going was rough, deciding that whatever else might happen he just couldn't see himself running away. "Should a man like me run?"

Escapism is corroding families, individuals, society and the church. Consider the church specifically. The world encourages us to change from one denomination to another. There are problems in every denomination, in every local church. We must refuse to run. We can't run out every time the going gets rough. By now, you'd think we would be fed up with the illusion of the easy path. The bias today is that we shouldn't have to face unpleasant things on the assumption that nobody should be challenged to do anything he doesn't like. Everything should be made as easy as possible for everybody. If you don't like it, you leave it.

The Bible talks about life as it really is. It talks about hardships to be endured, crosses to be carried, evils to be overcome, tribulations to be triumphed in and plows to put your hand to from which there's no turning back. Nowhere is there the faintest hint that life was to be easy or that you can dodge it or run out on any of it. It is all there: drudgery, difficulty and even sorrow.

We're made to stand up to difficulty. We're to wrestle with it, see it through and stay with it until we see the Lord glorified. You know what you're facing at work. You know the realities in your home, presbytery and church. You may want to run. Stand up to it, face it, and give up your right to quit. Make a permanent choice. Settle once and for all that for you quitting is unthinkable.

God doesn't quit. He doesn't run. That's what Gethsemane means. That's what Calvary means. Because you belong to God and were adopted as sons and daughters of the Most High, you can never run. Stay and rebuild your life, your home, your church, the Church. Stay until all resounds with the truth of God's Word in Jesus Christ.

Almighty God, forgive me for the ways I cheapen the gospel. Thank you for staying and fighting for me in Gethsemane and on the cross. Keep me true to you and seeking your best in the tough times. I pray that your will be done in my life. I pray these things in the strong name of Jesus Christ, my Rock and Redeemer. Amen.

※

For He Himself is our peace,
who has made the two one
and has destroyed the barrier,
the dividing wall of hostility.

Ephesians 2:14

Lucy and Linus have a turkey wishbone, and they're about to make their wishes and pull it. Lucy, the bossy older sister, presumes to lecture Linus on the rules of the game.

"Do I have to say my wish out loud?" he asks.

"Of course," Lucy replies; "if you don't say it out loud it won't come true." Then she proceeds to make her wish, closing her eyes tight. "I wish for four new sweaters, a new bike, a new pair of skates, a new dress and a hundred dollars."

Linus then shuts his eyes, grasps the wishbone, and says, "I wish for a long life for all my friends, for world peace, and for great advancements in medical research."

At this Lucy grabs the wishbone and throws it away. "That's the trouble with you, Linus," she says. "You're always spoiling everything."

It does spoil things, doesn't it, when into our self-centered and materialistic and fractured world someone comes who forgets their own needs and looks to the needs of others. Magnified by millions of times, that's the effect that Jesus had on the game that sinful mankind has been playing. His radical mission was to bring together a world that is deeply divided. And we are, indeed, people divided. We humans divide ourselves by nations, ethnic groups, politics, races and loyalties. Our communities become separated and fractured. Marriages and families divide by selfishness and self-interest.

The ground-breaking, culture-changing work of Jesus is described for us in Ephesians 2. Our Lord came to tear down the walls, to make out of His Church a new humanity of people who are wall-breakers. He led the way, showing us how to bust apart the sin that separates us. He calls us to do likewise.

> Go out into the world in peace, have courage, hold on to what is good, return no man evil for evil. Strengthen the faint-hearted, support the weak, help the suffering, honor all men and women. Love and serve the Lord, rejoicing in the power of the Holy Spirit.

One man who was a wall-breaker was named Joe Gordon. He was a star baseball player for the Cleveland Indians. It was 1947, when his career was in its prime. The Indians that year brought to the major leagues a rookie named Larry Doby, the first African-American to play in the American League. Many fans, many opponents on the other teams, and even some of his own teammates were resistant to Doby. He felt the silent treatment, the shunning, the isolation – and it added to the natural nervousness and stress that any rookie ballplayer feels. In his first at-bat on opening day, Doby was a jangle of nerves. He swung and missed on the first three pitches that were thrown his way – and missed each by at least a foot. With boos cascading on his shoulders, he slouched back to the dugout and sat in the corner dejectedly. Gordon, the team's leading power hitter, was up next.

The pitcher was one that he usually blasted out of the park. But in this at-bat Joe Gordon swung and missed three times – each by at least two feet. He returned to the dugout, walked past all the other players on the bench, and sat next to Larry Doby. No one dared ask if Joe Gordon had struck out deliberately. But Larry Doby now knew he had a friend on the team. As long as they played together after that, Doby would pick up Gordon's glove on the way out of the dugout and toss it to him. Larry Doby went on to become one of the league's strongest hitters. What kind of an impact did one wall-breaker have on him?

That's what breaking down walls can do. St. Paul tells us it was the reason why Christ came to us. Is there a wall somewhere in your life that your Lord wants you to tear down? Do you need to forgive and forget something that was done to you? Do you need to take the first step of apologizing and asking forgiveness of someone who may be alienated from you? Is there someone who is different, neglected, excluded or pushed aside whom you need to reach out and touch?

Robert Frost understood at least this much of the Christian Gospel when he wrote, "Something there is that doesn't love a wall, that wants it down." Jesus saw the walls of His day and wanted them down. Ultimately He surrendered His own life that the greatest wall of all – the one separating sinful men and women from a Holy God – could be removed by His own blood. And once we are reconciled to our Creator, He wants us to carry on the work of reconciliation with those around us.

My favorite scriptural benediction, which I have pronounced as a pastor before the bowed heads of congregations on many occasions, is the charge to be wall-breakers. It goes like this:

> Go out into the world in peace,
> have courage,
> hold on to what is good,

return no man evil for evil.
Strengthen the faint-hearted,
support the weak,
help the suffering,
honor all men and women.
Love and serve the Lord,
rejoicing in the power of the Holy Spirit.
May that calling inspire each of us, this day and every day.

Heavenly Father, thank you that your Son broke down the wall
that separated me from You. Because I am one with you, I know
I am also called to be one with all of your other children. Help me
to see the walls that may be separating me from others, and
help me by your grace to break them down and to
connect with others in love. Amen.

✳

When he had said this,
Jesus called in a loud voice,
"Lazarus, come out!"

John 11:43

During the dark days before the Civil War, slaves in the South had little to hope for. They had been torn from their homes and families in Africa. Their families were repeatedly shattered as husband and wife and children could be sold off in different directions. They turned to the words of Ezekiel to give them hope that someday they, too, might be free, might again be a people. And so they sang that rollicking spiritual: *Dem bones, dem bones, dem dry bones. Now hear the word of the Lord. The foot bone connected to the ankle bone, the ankle bone connected to the leg bone, the leg bone connected to the thigh bone. Now hear the word of the Lord.*

God gave Ezekiel a vision of a valley of bones. These bones had qualities that represented the situation of Ezekiel's people. They were dry, indicating deadness. There appeared to be no hope that they would be revived. And the bones were separated from one another, just as the people of Israel were scattered across the earth. Then God told Ezekiel to prophesy. And Ezekiel prophesied. And when he did, there was a noise, a rattling sound, and the bones came together, bone to bone. Then tendons and flesh appeared on the bones and skin covered them, but there was no breath in them. Then God told Ezekiel to prophesy to the wind. The wind, representing the Spirit of God, began to blow. And the bones began to breathe. *Dem bones, dem bones, dem dry bones …* Then God said, "Therefore prophesy, and say to them, 'Thus says the Lord God: I am going to open your graves, and bring you up from your graves, O my people; and I will bring you back to the land of Israel. And you shall know that I am the Lord, when I open your graves, and bring you up from your graves, O my people. I will put my spirit within you, and you shall live, and I will place you on your own soil; then you shall know that I, the Lord, have spoken and will act, says the Lord." The people of Israel had God's promise. Those dry bones would live again.

Now, let's move ahead a few hundred years. Mary and Martha expected that Jesus would come immediately when he received word that their brother Lazarus, Jesus' good friend, was seriously ill. Jesus had been in their home many times. They knew he loved them and they waited expectantly for his arrival. But Jesus lingered where he was and did not come until Lazarus had died and been in the tomb for four days. The home of Mary and Martha was like the valley of dry bones when Jesus did arrive. The sisters' hearts were breaking; their spirits were low. Mary said to Jesus, "Lord, if you had been here, my brother would not have died." Jesus was touched by this and asked, "Where have you laid him?" They told him to come and see. Jesus began to weep. The Jews said, "See how he loved him!" Then Jesus came to the tomb. It was a cave, and a stone was lying against it. Jesus said, "Take away the stone." Martha said, "Lord, already there is a stench because he has been dead four days." Jesus said to her, "Did I not tell you that if you believed, you would see the glory of God?" So they took away the stone. And Jesus looked upward and said, "Father, I thank you for having heard me. I knew that you always hear me, but I have said this for the sake of the crowd standing here, so that they may believe that you sent me." When he had said this, he cried with a loud voice, "Lazarus, come out!" The dead man came out, his hands and feet bound with strips of cloth and his face wrapped in a cloth. Jesus said to them, "Unbind him, and let him go." *Dem bones, dem bones, dem dry bones …* Jesus had brought the dry bones of Lazarus to life again. *Now hear the word of the Lord.*

Lazarus had been in the tomb for four days. We can be sure that Lazarus was morally, ethically, physically, absolutely, positively, undeniably, and reliably dead! One scholar notes that there was a Jewish belief that the soul of the departed hovered around the body for three days hoping to return, but when decomposition set in it would leave. Lazarus had been dead four days when Jesus arrived at his home, so no one could doubt that Lazarus was totally, completely dead. But Christ gave him new life. He called him forth from the tomb and set him free. There are some things we need to see about this miracle of our Lord.

We need to understand this miracle had a specific purpose – that both God and the Son of God would be glorified. Jesus was moved by Mary's and Martha's grief. After all, he loved them. But this is not why he raised Lazarus. The resurrection of Lazarus was not for Lazarus' benefit. After all, he died as a friend of Jesus. His destiny was taken care of. Neither was it for Mary's and Martha's benefit. Lazarus' resurrection was temporary at best. It is not recorded, but doubtless Lazarus died again. If Jesus raised people because of his love and consideration for people left behind, then all the cemeteries would be empty, for Jesus loves all of us who are confronted with the loss of a loved one. No, in the Bible miracles take place for a specific purpose. Jesus stated the purpose of this particular miracle – that both the Father and the Son might be glorified. This story affirms Christ's power over life and death. In fact, that is how the Son is glorified, by this demonstration of his power over the grave. The Bible is unequivocal. Jesus has power over death. This is why the story of the raising of Lazarus appears in John's gospel. It is to say to us that Christ has power over both life and death.

Jesus Christ has the power to give us new life. You and I may spend our entire lives and never see a miracle like the kind of miracles the Bible describes. But we can experience a miracle. Christ comes into our lives and gives us a new heart, a new spirit, a new outlook, a new destiny.

A nurse, before listening to the child's chest, would plug the stethoscope into his ears and let him listen to his own heart. The child's eyes would always light up with awe. But she never got a response to equal four-year-old David's. Gently she tucked the stethoscope in his ears and placed the disk over his heart. "Listen," she said, "what do you suppose that is?" He drew his eyebrows together in a puzzled line and looked up as if lost in the mystery of the strange tap-tap-tapping deep in his chest. Then his face broke out in a wondrous grin. "Who's knocking? Is that Jesus knocking?"

Friend, is Jesus knocking on the door to your heart this day? This is the day to bring dead bones to life, either through regeneration for salvation or through confession, repentance and forgiveness. *Dem bones, dem bones, dem dry bones.*

Oh God, I hear your voice telling me to come out of the grave. I am coming out. Thank you, Father, for giving me living bones. In Jesus' name I pray, Amen.

✺

Wait for the LORD; be strong and take heart,
and wait for the LORD.

Psalm 27:14

God gives to us His special creatures many wonderful gifts, which are ours from our birth or early years. Some of us are gifted with the ability to play or sing music, or we have a natural gift for art, or we have good hand-eye coordination to play sports and games. But there are some things that none of us do naturally. Certain skills in life have to be learned, and they are always difficult for us. One of those is the skill of waiting patiently. None of us likes to do it, and none of us does it with ease. It's hard to wait. But it's an essential part of the Christian life. And some of us are struggling to master it right now.

At times God speaks to us loudly and clearly. At other times it feels as if He is silent. If we are stirred to wonder by God's voice, we are baffled by His silence. Today we are going to think about how to listen to the silence.

We all live in the same world. Though we may vary in ages, in nationalities, in net worth, in professional backgrounds, and in where we've lived, still we go through the same experiences in varying degrees. And whether we react to the times of God's silence in doubt or in faith depends on something within ourselves. Some react in bitterness. But others have learned that the silence of heaven is not a harsh silence. These blessed ones have caught a glimmer of the meaning of silence. They have seen stars shining in the night sky that they would never have noticed in the bright daylight.

If we come to see that our true purpose here on earth isn't happiness but holiness, we realize that some measure of struggle is inevitable. How could we develop courage without facing danger? How could we learn sympathy for others' pain if we've never suffered ourselves? How could we become tenderhearted without at times having our hearts torn? How could we learn to depend on God if our own strength were always sufficient?

An American couple went to England to celebrate their 25th anniversary. Both the man and his wife were collectors of fine pottery and china. While touring in Sussex they passed a little china shop. As they browsed, they both noticed a small teacup on the top shelf. "May I see that cup?" the man asked the proprietor. "I've never seen one quite like it. It's beautiful." As he held the cup in his hand, amazingly the teacup spoke.

"I haven't always been a teacup. There was a time when I was just a lump of red clay. My master took me and rolled me and pressed me down, over and over. I cried out 'Leave me alone,' but he only smiled and said, 'Not yet.' Then I was placed on a spinning wheel, and I was spun around and around. I screamed 'Stop … I'm getting dizzy.' The master only shook his head and said, 'Not yet.' Then he put me in an oven. I've never felt such heat, and I wondered why he was burning me. I yelled and pounded on the door of the oven, and could see him through the small window just shake his head as his lips formed the words 'Not yet.' Finally he opened the door, took me out, and put me on a shelf to cool. 'This is much better,' I thought. 'At last my ordeal is over.' But it wasn't.

"Suddenly the master took me and began to brush me with paint all over, and the fumes were horrible, and I started to gag. 'Please stop!' I cried. But he shook his head and said, 'Not yet.' Then he put me back into the oven, and this time it was twice as hot. I pleaded for relief, but saw him again shake his head. 'Not yet.' Then I knew there was no hope for me. I was doomed. I'd never make it. I was ready to give up, when suddenly the oven door opened again, and he placed me on a shelf. An hour later he held a mirror and said, 'Now look at yourself.' And I did. And I said, 'That's not me. It couldn't be. I'm beautiful.'

"The master then explained, 'I know it was hard to be rolled and patted so forcefully, but it was the only way to soften you. I know it was dizzying to be spun around, but if I stopped you would not have been properly shaped. I know that the oven was hot, but if I hadn't put you in the fire you would have cracked. I know the fumes were bad as I brushed you, but if you hadn't been painted there would be no color in your life. And if I hadn't put you back in the oven, the color would not have lasted. Now you're finished. You are beautiful. You're what I had in mind when I first thought of you.'"

When the Scriptures whisper to us repeatedly, "Wait for the Lord," it is for our good. The Master has a purpose and plan for all of us.

Lord, it is hard to wait upon You. My natural instinct is to be impatient. At times I even feel fear or panic when I'm required to wait. But I want to learn to trust in You and be patient. I believe that You do have a purpose for my life, and that You even use painful and confusing and trying experiences to mold and shape me into the person You want me to be. Help me today to wait patiently for Your will to be done in my life. Amen.

✳

I tell you the truth, no one can enter the kingdom
of God unless he is born of water and the Spirit.
Flesh gives birth to flesh, but the Spirit gives birth
to spirit.

John 3:5-6

We all instinctively resist change, especially in
ourselves. And if we have to change, we'd rather
make it as superficial as possible, leaving our real
selves the same. But God's work in our lives is to change us deep
down, change us within, and change us from the inside out. This
was the shocking announcement he made to the religious professional Nicodemus on that quiet night in Jerusalem when they had
their unforgettable one-on-one conversation.

It was a small jazz club off Bourbon Street in the French
Quarter of New Orleans. A devoted clientele frequented it, and
up-and-coming musicians were eager to perform there. The
man who had owned the club for many years went into a period
of declining health and hospitalization, and finally died. During
his long illness the club had been neglected. A new owner
purchased the club. He was primarily interested in making
money from the bar, but much less concerned about the quality
of the music. The jazz artists performing in the club repeatedly
complained to the new owner that the piano was not up to par
and needed to be fixed. "Fine," the owner said one evening. The
next day he bought a can of cheap paint at a hardware store and
painted the piano. That should satisfy those spoiled musicians,

he thought. But painting the piano was just a superficial change. It didn't make it sound any better. The outer paint didn't change the problems within.

Our human nature is continually whispering to us that it should be enough to put a coat of paint on the old piano, rather than doing the more costly work of really fixing what's wrong. Nicodemus was apparently looking for some minor or cosmetic changes to improve his life a bit, and he thought that the itinerant preacher from Nazareth might have a few suggestions. What this prominent man received was far more than he had bargained for. Jesus told him that what was needed was a radical change within, a spiritual birth. And this was not something Nicodemus could do for himself. "Flesh gives birth to flesh." Our human efforts can simply produce fresh coats of paint on the surface. Only "the Spirit gives birth to spirit."

> If we truly want Christ to be our Lord, we need to be willing to let Him do His work and change us within. We can't just play it safe. We can't be content to slap a coat of paint on the piano. We have to let Him inside – to tune us, to change the inner workings, to make us new. This is the "new birth" the Bible tells us is essential in order to "enter the kingdom of God."

Father Henri Nouwen reflects on the story of Nicodemus, and reveals his own struggles to let the Spirit do His work within. "I tell myself I love Jesus, but I want to hold onto my old friends, even when they don't lead me closer to Him. I tell myself I love Jesus, but I want to hold on to my own independence, even when that independence brings me no real freedom. I tell myself I love Jesus, but I do not want to lose the respect of my professional colleagues, even though I know they can't help me grow spiritually. I tell myself I love Jesus, but I don't want to give up my plans, even when those plans crowd Him out of my schedule. I guess I'm more like Nicodemus than I thought I was."

If we truly want Christ to be our Lord, we need to be willing to let Him do His work and change us within. We can't just play it safe. We can't be content to slap a coat of paint on the piano. We have to let Him inside – to tune us, to change the inner workings, to make us new. This is the "new birth" the Bible tells us is essential in order to "enter the kingdom of God."

And we need to repeatedly give Him permission to keep on changing us within, long after we are spiritually reborn. It's a never-completed process until that day when we will be with Him forever and see Him as He truly is. If you are struggling with some problem in your life right now, perhaps you are trying to keep control. Perhaps you are attempting to fix things by painting the old piano. Jesus wants you to allow Him to make deep and profound changes from within. He wants to take control. Will you yield to the Spirit to have His way in you?

Jesus, I confess that I am like Nicodemus. I prefer to keep you at a safe distance, rather than completely abandoning myself to you. But I truly want you to be my Lord, and to make me into the person you want me to be. Please take control and change me within, by the power of your Spirit. Amen.

✸

For He has rescued us from the dominion of
darkness and brought us into the kingdom of
the Son He loves, in whom we have redemption,
the forgiveness of sins.

Colossians 1:13-14

In Portugal there is a very unusual monastery. It's perched high
on a 300-foot cliff. You can only reach the monastery by a
terrifying ride in a swaying basket. The basket is pulled up the
cliff by a single rope, as several of the sturdy brothers strain and
pull together. One American tourist got nervous about halfway
up the cliff. He noticed that the rope seemed very old and frayed.
"How often do you change this rope?" he called up to the monks.
"Whenever it breaks," they shouted back.

Some of us get to feeling at times like we're in that kind of
precarious situation. The basket is swaying and the rope seems
frayed and in danger of pulling apart. It is regrettably common, in
our busy and stressed-out world, for our home lives and families
and marriages to get to the breaking point. Relationships are strained,
even to the point of hurtful words, violent actions and emotional
wounds. And when our homes and marriages become battlefields,
the damage can be lasting – passed on to the next generation.

If there are broken relationships in your home, or in your
work environment or social setting, perhaps you are feeling a
longing today for God to bring some healing and reconciliation.
Thankfully, the path to healing is marked out for us in scripture.

Paul's letter to the Colossians points the way. The first step to reconciliation with others is to be reconciled in the most vital, important and eternal relationship of all: between you and your God. This new beginning is made available to all of us. And all we have to do is receive it.

Notice that our true condition apart from Christ is clearly identified: we all live, in our natural state, in "the dominion of darkness." But we have been "rescued" from that. This word was used of the unexpected relief a besieged city would have from an army coming to drive away its oppressors. It is the word used of a prisoner who had been given the death sentence and then granted clemency and pardon. The dramatic Good News is that Christ has broken the power of the negative over your life. You are no longer bound by old patterns and habits, no longer caught in a cycle of getting even and settling scores. This deliverance is a gift, something we could never earn. And it brings us new hope.

> And once we have received Christ and His power into our lives, Paul goes on in the rest of the letter to the Colossians to talk about how to live in that new reality. "So then, just as you received Christ Jesus as Lord, continue to live in Him."

Rather than changing our outer circumstances, He changes us within. It's tempting for us to plead, "Please, Lord, transfer me out of this home ... give me a new husband [or wife or parents]." God instead works an inner transfer of our hearts and minds from the dominion of darkness to the kingdom of light.

And once we have received Christ and His power into our lives, Paul goes on in the rest of the letter to the Colossians to talk about how to live in that new reality. "So then, just as you received Christ Jesus as Lord, continue to live in Him."

Perhaps you're feeling lately a bit like the tourist in the basket on the face of the cliff: wondering if the old frayed rope will hold you. I promise you that there is One who promises to uphold you and keep your rope from breaking. He wants to bless you and your homes and all your relationships, and to help you live in the new reality of the Kingdom of Light.

Lord, you have assured me that my Savior's death has worked to bring me out of the dominion of darkness and into your kingdom. I receive His death for me, and I claim His power to make my life new. Bless me with your Spirit, that I might live in harmony and reconciliation with others as you lead me daily. Amen.

※

"What shall I do, then,
with Jesus who is called Christ?" Pilate asked.
They all answered, "Crucify Him!"
"Why? What crime has he committed?" asked Pilate.
But they shouted all the louder, "Crucify Him!"

Matthew 27:22-23

Mob scenes are always ugly, and they show human nature at its worst and most frightening. Some of us remember the dangerous riots that erupted in major cities in the 1960's; the smashed windows, looted stores and burning cars were the worst nightmare for a police department. We recall stories from the Old West about lynch mobs of vigilantes, who sometimes would hang an innocent man without due process. We recall stories from the Deep South about marauding bands of hooded KKK members attacking innocent blacks. The annals of military history tell many tales of out-of-control conquering armies that inflicted innocent populations, pillaging and burning and raping and murdering civilians. But the mob scene described in our text from Matthew 27 may very well be ranked as the darkest moment for the human race.

Self-esteem has become the cure-all elixir offered by modern pop psychology. "I'm okay and you're okay." Feel good about yourself. We're teaching generations of children that they're all special, they all deserves trophies and awards for everything they do, and nothing they ever do is wrong. Understanding psychologists and counselors assure people that their problems and dysfunctions are not their fault but can be blamed on others. As Dr. Karl Menninger asked, "Whatever became of sin?" We no longer want to even hear the word.

But the Gospel story puts the lie to our delusions that we're all good people. It reveals in stark and unmistakable relief the dark side and the sinful nature of humanity. I would like to ask the glib admirers of man and the apologists for mankind's blamelessness to look closely at the events leading to the cross. It was not demons but ordinary men and women like you and me who gave in to their worst impulses and shouted, "Crucify Him!" Though we are tempted to point the finger of blame at them, we must humbly admit that we, too, were there in a sense … and that our sins contributed to sending Christ to the cross.

A preacher who tells people the truth about our nature will never earn popularity points. A wave of optimistic and romantic humanism swept across Europe in the late 19th and early 20th centuries (before the horrors of a world war ended their naive optimism that mankind was evolving towards moral perfection). Charles Spurgeon, a pastor in London and one who drew his understanding of the nature of man not from the popular sentiments but from the Bible, one Sunday quoted from his pulpit a popular contemporary writer from the humanist movement. "Mankind longs for pure virtue," this author said. "If only we could see it embodied, we would all embrace and follow it." Spurgeon then scoffed. "Perfect virtue once came in the flesh," he said, "and our response was to cry in a unified voice, 'Crucify him!'"

In what ways was the act of crucifying the Lord of Glory a heinous crime?

First, because Christ was pure goodness in its most attractive form, yet we rejected it. His character was matchless and unimpeachable. No one was ever able to claim with any evidence or substance that Jesus had ever done a single thing wrong in His entire life. All His actions were pure, His motives impeccable and perfect. He willingly chose poverty over riches, and never owned a home or anything of substance. Rather than acquiring and getting for Himself, He relentlessly gave. Rather than seizing power, He declined it.

> Why is it valuable for us to reflect on our greatest crime – the evil of the human race's rejection of its Savior – and our complicity in it? We do so not to destroy our self-esteem, punish ourselves, or wallow in our guilt. Rather, we reflect on this horrible deed in order that we might fall to our knees in repentance and true humility.

Second, the crime of the crucifixion was a heinous evil because Christ was our best friend, yet we turned our backs on Him. He saved others, but He did not speak a sound or lift a word to defend Himself before His judges. Yet even His closest friends deserted Him to protect themselves. He healed the sick but surrendered His own body to be brutally destroyed. He granted forgiveness and grace to all He met, but we had no mercy to spare for Him.

And third, our rejection was the blackest of crimes because Christ was our greatest teacher, but we closed our minds to His truths. He taught mankind the deepest of all truths, and yet did so in ways that even a child could understand. Put together all the great sages of the past (from Socrates to Plato to Aristotle, from Confucius to Cicero): the sum total of all they taught for the promotion of real happiness and true goodness pales in comparison to the Sermon on the Mount given by Jesus. Its wisdom outweighs the wisdom of all the great empires. And yet His message was rejected by those who heard it with their own ears and should have embraced it.

Why is it valuable for us to reflect on our greatest crime – the evil of the human race's rejection of its Savior – and our complicity in it? We do so not to destroy our self-esteem, punish ourselves, or wallow in our guilt. Rather, we reflect on this horrible deed in order that we might fall to our knees in repentance and true humility. Had you and I been there on that fateful Friday centuries ago in Jerusalem, had we stood in the midst of the sweaty and feverish mob, whipped into a frenzy and caught up in the peer pressure of our neighbors, goaded on by the leading clergymen of the day, can we honestly be certain that we would not have added our voices to the rest of the mob in shouting "Crucify Him!"

We return to Good Friday each year to remember who we are, and to remember how much we need forgiveness and redemption. We bow our knees again when we contemplate human sin and God's sacrifice. And when we've done so, we rise with a different cry on our lips: not "crucify Him" but "crown Him!"

Thank you, Jesus, for your sacrifice on the cross for us, though we are unworthy of your mercy. We know what we are made of, and we know that we might have joined in the crowd that called for your crucifixion. Keep us ever humble, and ever mindful of our weakness and our need of your grace. Amen.

✳